SRA

LANGUAGE
for
LEARNING

Siegfried Engelmann
Jean Osborn

Answer Key

A Direct Instruction Program

McGraw Hill **SRA**

Columbus, OH

SRAonline.com

 SRA

Send all inquiries to this address:
SRA/McGraw-Hill
4400 Easton Commons
Columbus, OH 43219

ISBN: 978-0-07-609439-4
MHID: 0-07-609439-1

2 3 4 5 6 7 8 9 MAZ 13 12 11 10 09 08

The *McGraw·Hill* Companies

Lesson 1   Name _____

brown   green

Touch each object. Ask, "What is this?" Tell child to touch each object as you name it.

X X X X X

Touch a cross-out mark. Ask, "What is this?"

LESSON 1 • SIDE 1

Lesson 2   Name _____

orange   blue

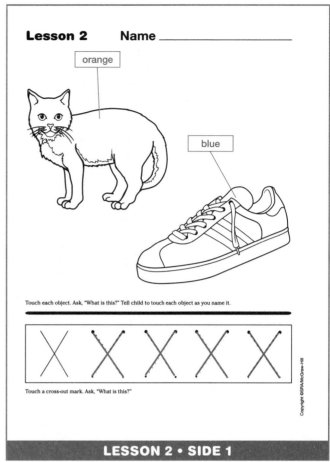

Touch each object. Ask, "What is this?" Tell child to touch each object as you name it.

X X X X X

Touch a cross-out mark. Ask, "What is this?"

LESSON 2 • SIDE 1

Lesson 3   Name _____

brown   green

Touch each object. Ask, "What is this?" Tell child to touch each object as you name it.

X X X X X

Touch a cross-out mark. Ask, "What is this?"

LESSON 3 • SIDE 1

Lesson 4   Name _____

brown   yellow

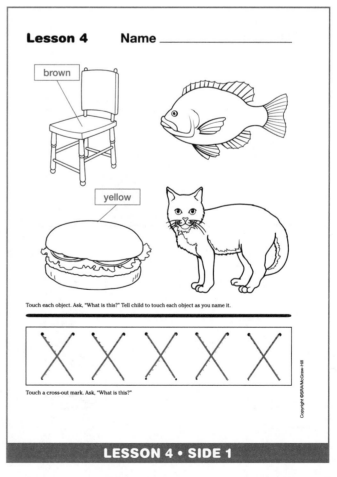

Touch each object. Ask, "What is this?" Tell child to touch each object as you name it.

X X X X X

Touch a cross-out mark. Ask, "What is this?"

LESSON 4 • SIDE 1

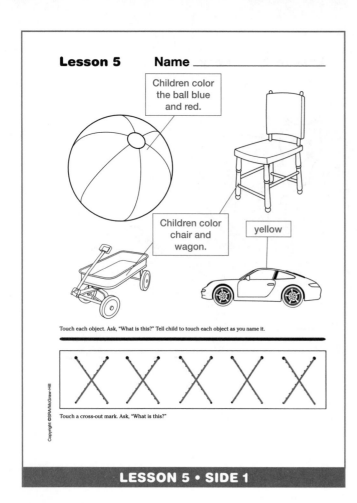

Lesson 5   Name _____

Children color the ball blue and red.

Children color chair and wagon.

yellow

Touch each object. Ask, "What is this?" Tell child to touch each object as you name it.

Touch a cross-out mark. Ask, "What is this?"

LESSON 5 • SIDE 1

Lesson 6   Name _____

"Touch the cross-out mark you drew in the box."

Children color the objects.

Touch each object. Ask, "What is this?" Tell child to touch each object as you name it.

Tell child to name each object. "Show me the line for the boys." Repeat for dogs and cars.

LESSON 6 • SIDE 1

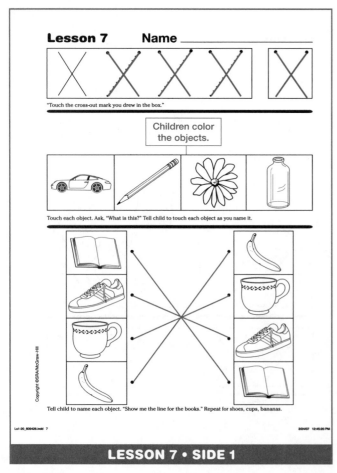

Lesson 7   Name _____

"Touch the cross-out mark you drew in the box."

Children color the objects.

Touch each object. Ask, "What is this?" Tell child to touch each object as you name it.

Tell child to name each object. "Show me the line for the books." Repeat for shoes, cups, bananas.

Ls1-20_609428.indd 7   2/24/07 12:45:20 PM

LESSON 7 • SIDE 1

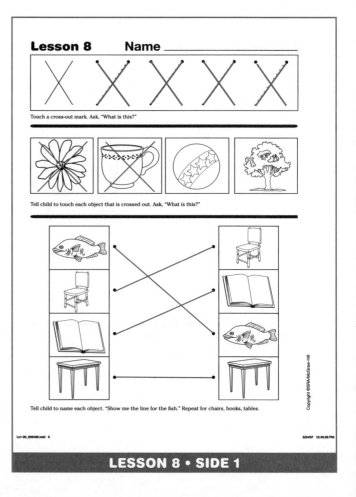

Lesson 8   Name _____

Touch a cross-out mark. Ask, "What is this?"

Tell child to touch each object that is crossed out. Ask, "What is this?"

Tell child to name each object. "Show me the line for the fish." Repeat for chairs, books, tables.

Ls1-20_609428.indd 8   2/24/07 12:45:25 PM

LESSON 8 • SIDE 1

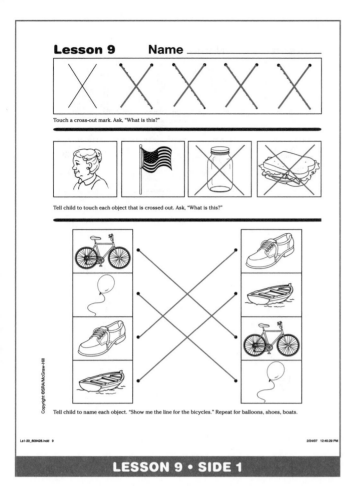

Lesson 9 Name _____

Touch a cross-out mark. Ask, "What is this?"

Tell child to touch each object that is crossed out. Ask, "What is this?"

Tell child to name each object. "Show me the line for the bicycles." Repeat for balloons, shoes, boats.

Ls1-20_609428.indd 9 2/24/07 12:45:29 PM

LESSON 9 • SIDE 1

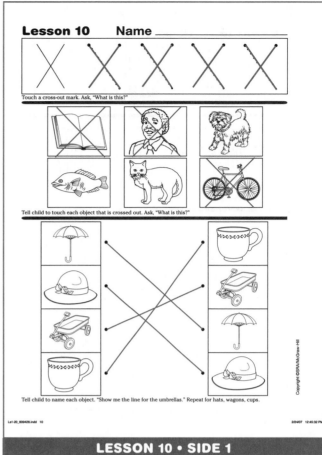

Lesson 10 Name _____

Touch a cross-out mark. Ask, "What is this?"

Tell child to touch each object that is crossed out. Ask, "What is this?"

Tell child to name each object. "Show me the line for the umbrellas." Repeat for hats, wagons, cups.

Ls1-20_609428.indd 10 2/24/07 12:45:32 PM

LESSON 10 • SIDE 1

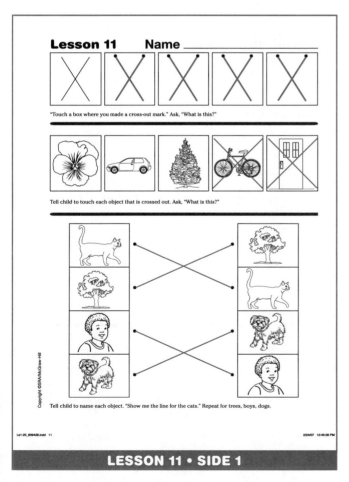

Lesson 11 Name _____

"Touch a box where you made a cross-out mark." Ask, "What is this?"

Tell child to touch each object that is crossed out. Ask, "What is this?"

Tell child to name each object. "Show me the line for the cats." Repeat for trees, boys, dogs.

Ls1-20_609428.indd 11 2/24/07 12:45:36 PM

LESSON 11 • SIDE 1

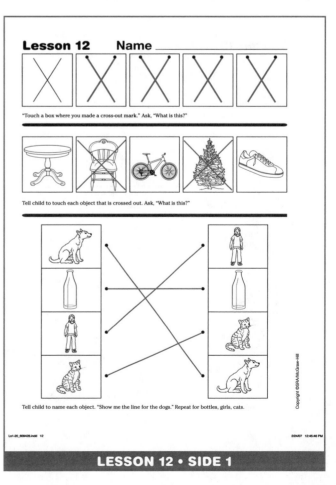

Lesson 12 Name _____

"Touch a box where you made a cross-out mark." Ask, "What is this?"

Tell child to touch each object that is crossed out. Ask, "What is this?"

Tell child to name each object. "Show me the line for the dogs." Repeat for bottles, girls, cats.

Ls1-20_609428.indd 12 2/24/07 12:45:46 PM

LESSON 12 • SIDE 1

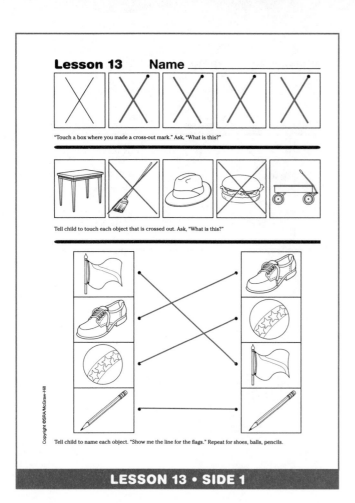

Lesson 13   Name _____

"Touch a box where you made a cross-out mark." Ask, "What is this?"

Tell child to touch each object that is crossed out. Ask, "What is this?"

Tell child to name each object. "Show me the line for the flags." Repeat for shoes, balls, pencils.

Copyright ©SRA/McGraw-Hill

LESSON 13 • SIDE 1

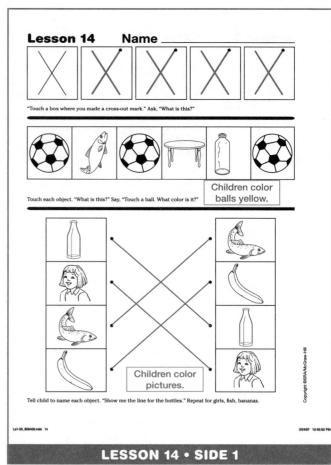

Lesson 14   Name _____

"Touch a box where you made a cross-out mark." Ask, "What is this?"

Children color balls yellow.

Touch each object. "What is this?" Say, "Touch a ball. What color is it?"

Children color pictures.

Tell child to name each object. "Show me the line for the bottles." Repeat for girls, fish, bananas.

Copyright ©SRA/McGraw-Hill

Ls1-20_609428.indd 14   2/24/07 12:45:52 PM

LESSON 14 • SIDE 1

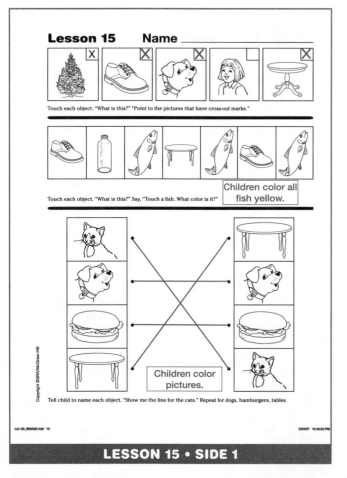

Lesson 15   Name _____

Touch each object. "What is this?" "Point to the pictures that have cross-out marks."

Children color all fish yellow.

Touch each object. "What is this?" Say, "Touch a fish. What color is it?"

Children color pictures.

Tell child to name each object. "Show me the line for the cats." Repeat for dogs, hamburgers, tables.

Copyright ©SRA/McGraw-Hill

Ls1-20_609428.indd 15   2/24/07 12:45:55 PM

LESSON 15 • SIDE 1

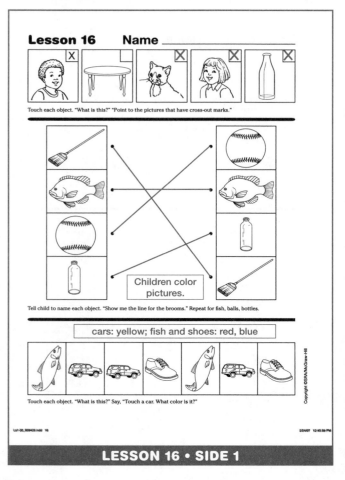

Lesson 16   Name _____

Touch each object. "What is this?" "Point to the pictures that have cross-out marks."

Children color pictures.

Tell child to name each object. "Show me the line for the brooms." Repeat for fish, balls, bottles.

cars: yellow; fish and shoes: red, blue

Touch each object. "What is this?" Say, "Touch a car. What color is it?"

Copyright ©SRA/McGraw-Hill

Ls1-20_609428.indd 16   2/24/07 12:45:59 PM

LESSON 16 • SIDE 1

4

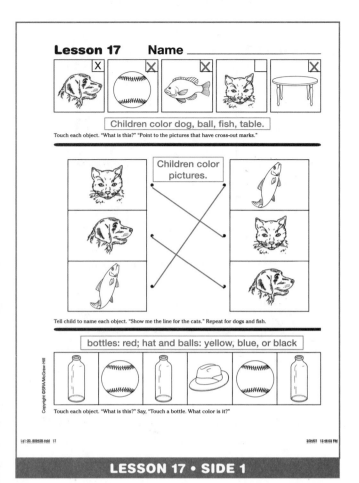

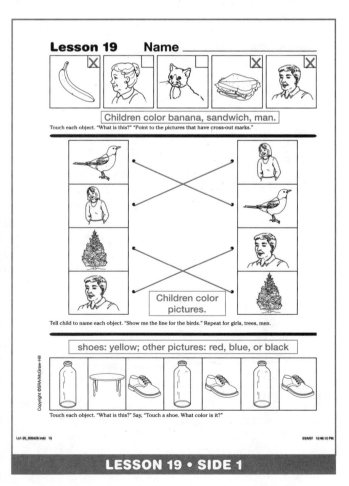

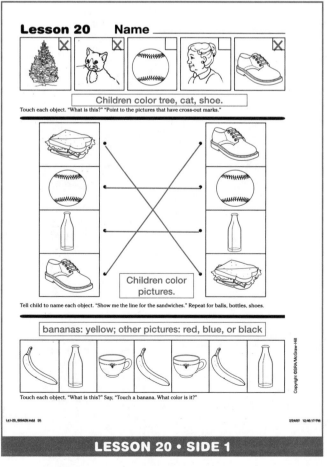

LESSON 17 • SIDE 1

LESSON 18 • SIDE 1

LESSON 19 • SIDE 1

LESSON 20 • SIDE 1

5

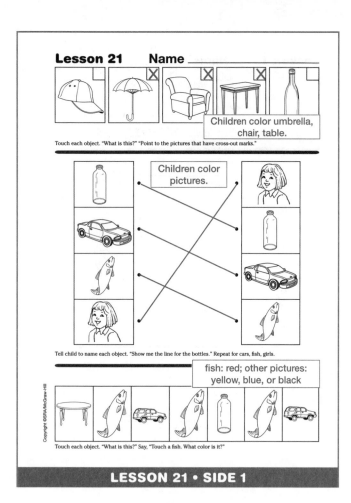

Lesson 21 Name _____

Children color umbrella, chair, table.

Touch each object. "What is this?" "Point to the pictures that have cross-out marks."

Children color pictures.

Tell child to name each object. "Show me the line for the bottles." Repeat for cars, fish, girls.

fish: red; other pictures: yellow, blue, or black

Touch each object. "What is this?" Say, "Touch a fish. What color is it?"

LESSON 21 • SIDE 1

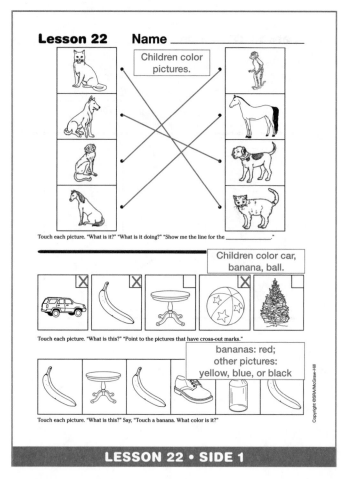

Lesson 22 Name _____

Children color pictures.

Touch each picture. "What is it?" "What is it doing?" "Show me the line for the _____."

Children color car, banana, ball.

Touch each picture. "What is this?" "Point to the pictures that have cross-out marks."

bananas: red; other pictures: yellow, blue, or black

Touch each picture. "What is this?" Say, "Touch a banana. What color is it?"

LESSON 22 • SIDE 1

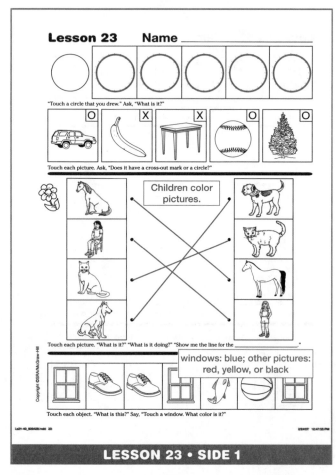

Lesson 23 Name _____

"Touch a circle that you drew." Ask, "What is it?"

Touch each picture. Ask, "Does it have a cross-out mark or a circle?"

Children color pictures.

Touch each picture. "What is it?" "What is it doing?" "Show me the line for the _____."

windows: blue; other pictures: red, yellow, or black

Touch each object. "What is this?" Say, "Touch a window. What color is it?"

LESSON 23 • SIDE 1

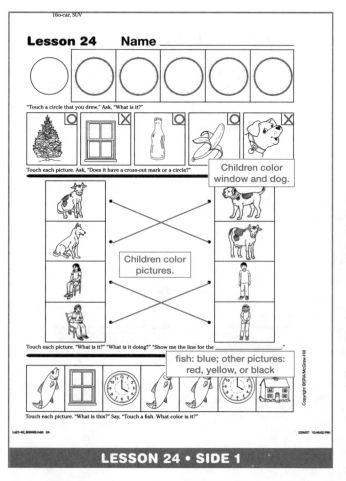

16o-car, SUV

Lesson 24 Name _____

"Touch a circle that you drew." Ask, "What is it?"

Touch each picture. Ask, "Does it have a cross-out mark or a circle?"

Children color window and dog.

Children color pictures.

Touch each picture. "What is it?" "What is it doing?" "Show me the line for the _____."

fish: blue; other pictures: red, yellow, or black

Touch each picture. "What is this?" Say, "Touch a fish. What color is it?"

LESSON 24 • SIDE 1

6

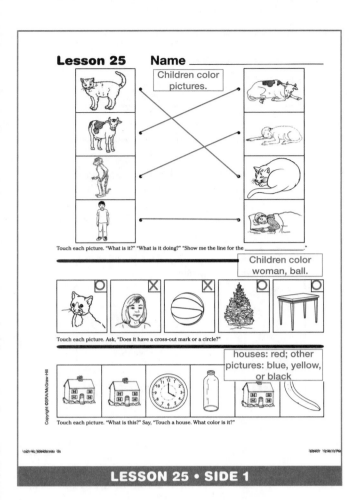

Lesson 25   Name _____

Children color pictures.

Touch each picture. "What is it?" "What is it doing?" "Show me the line for the _____."

Children color woman, ball.

Touch each picture. Ask, "Does it have a cross-out mark or a circle?"

houses: red; other pictures: blue, yellow, or black

Touch each picture. "What is this?" Say, "Touch a house. What color is it?"

Copyright ©SRA/McGraw-Hill

LESSON 25 • SIDE 1

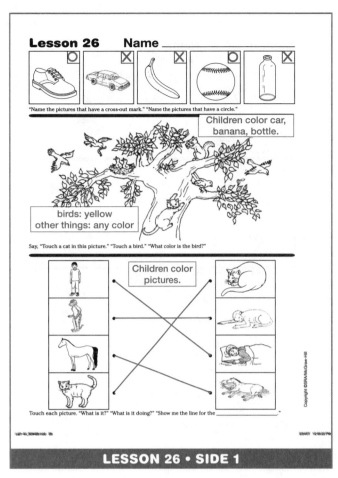

Lesson 26   Name _____

"Name the pictures that have a cross-out mark." "Name the pictures that have a circle."

Children color car, banana, bottle.

birds: yellow
other things: any color

Say, "Touch a cat in this picture." "Touch a bird." "What color is the bird?"

Children color pictures.

Touch each picture. "What is it?" "What is it doing?" "Show me the line for the _____."

Copyright ©SRA/McGraw-Hill

LESSON 26 • SIDE 1

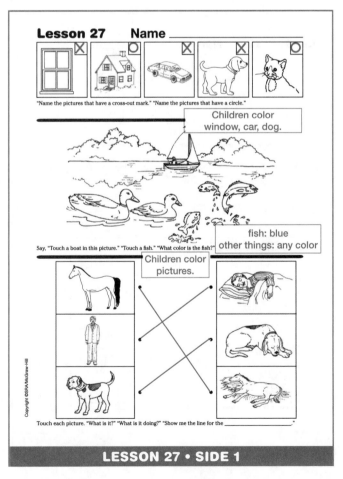

Lesson 27   Name _____

"Name the pictures that have a cross-out mark." "Name the pictures that have a circle."

Children color window, car, dog.

Say, "Touch a boat in this picture." "Touch a fish." "What color is the fish?"

fish: blue
other things: any color

Children color pictures.

Touch each picture. "What is it?" "What is it doing?" "Show me the line for the _____."

Copyright ©SRA/McGraw-Hill

LESSON 27 • SIDE 1

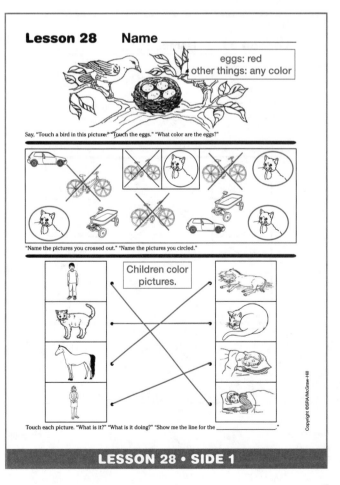

Lesson 28   Name _____

eggs: red
other things: any color

Say, "Touch a bird in this picture." "Touch the eggs." "What color are the eggs?"

"Name the pictures you crossed out." "Name the pictures you circled."

Children color pictures.

Touch each picture. "What is it?" "What is it doing?" "Show me the line for the _____."

Copyright ©SRA/McGraw-Hill

LESSON 28 • SIDE 1

7

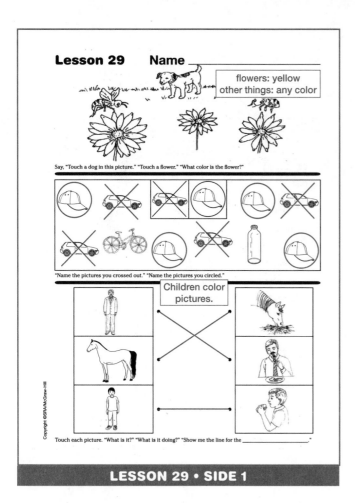

Lesson 29   Name _____

flowers: yellow
other things: any color

Say, "Touch a dog in this picture." "Touch a flower." "What color is the flower?"

"Name the pictures you crossed out." "Name the pictures you circled."

Children color pictures.

Touch each picture. "What is it?" "What is it doing?" "Show me the line for the _____."

LESSON 29 • SIDE 1

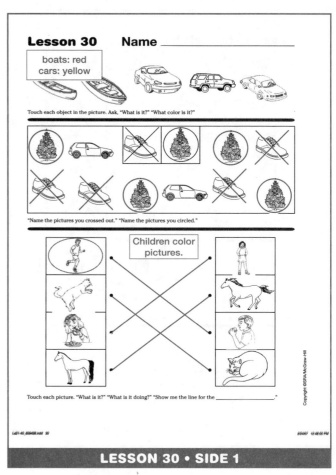

Lesson 30   Name _____

boats: red
cars: yellow

Touch each object in the picture. Ask, "What is it?" "What color is it?"

"Name the pictures you crossed out." "Name the pictures you circled."

Children color pictures.

Touch each picture. "What is it?" "What is it doing?" "Show me the line for the _____."

LESSON 30 • SIDE 1

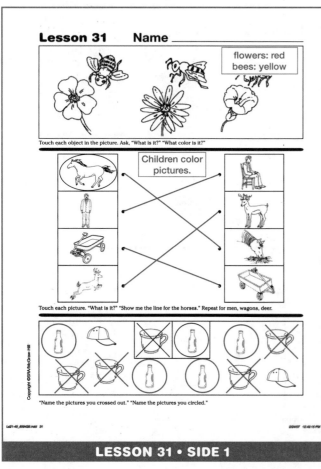

Lesson 31   Name _____

flowers: red
bees: yellow

Touch each object in the picture. Ask, "What is it?" "What color is it?"

Children color pictures.

Touch each picture. "What is it?" "Show me the line for the horses." Repeat for men, wagons, deer.

"Name the pictures you crossed out." "Name the pictures you circled."

LESSON 31 • SIDE 1

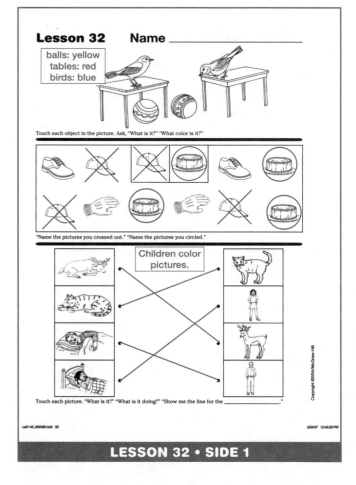

Lesson 32   Name _____

balls: yellow
tables: red
birds: blue

Touch each object in the picture. Ask, "What is it?" "What color is it?"

"Name the pictures you crossed out." "Name the pictures you circled."

Children color pictures.

Touch each picture. "What is it?" "What is it doing?" "Show me the line for the _____."

LESSON 32 • SIDE 1

8

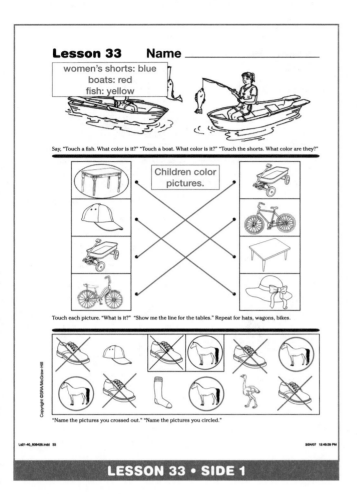

Lesson 33   Name _____

women's shorts: blue
boats: red
fish: yellow

Say, "Touch a fish. What color is it?" "Touch a boat. What color is it?" "Touch the shorts. What color are they?"

Children color pictures.

Touch each picture. "What is it?" "Show me the line for the tables." Repeat for hats, wagons, bikes.

"Name the pictures you crossed out." "Name the pictures you circled."

Copyright ©SRA/McGraw-Hill

Ls21-40_609428.indd 33   2/24/07 12:49:39 PM

LESSON 33 • SIDE 1

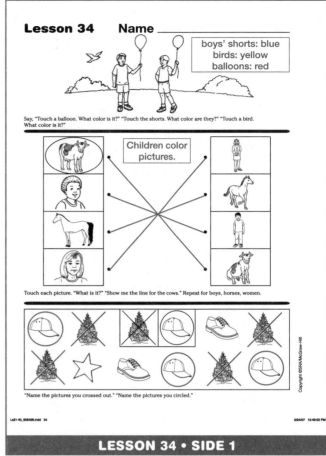

Lesson 34   Name _____

boys' shorts: blue
birds: yellow
balloons: red

Say, "Touch a balloon. What color is it?" "Touch the shorts. What color are they?" "Touch a bird. What color is it?"

Children color pictures.

Touch each picture. "What is it?" "Show me the line for the cows." Repeat for boys, horses, women.

"Name the pictures you crossed out." "Name the pictures you circled."

Copyright ©SRA/McGraw-Hill

Ls21-40_609428.indd 34   2/24/07 12:49:52 PM

LESSON 34 • SIDE 1

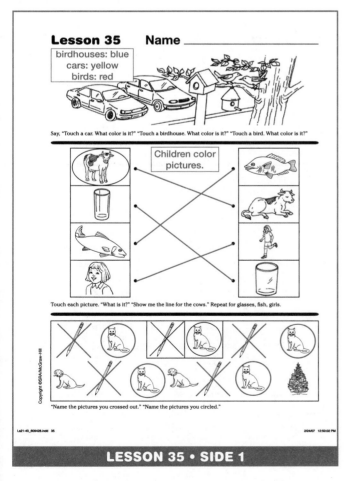

Lesson 35   Name _____

birdhouses: blue
cars: yellow
birds: red

Say, "Touch a car. What color is it?" "Touch a birdhouse. What color is it?" "Touch a bird. What color is it?"

Children color pictures.

Touch each picture. "What is it?" "Show me the line for the cows." Repeat for glasses, fish, girls.

"Name the pictures you crossed out." "Name the pictures you circled."

Copyright ©SRA/McGraw-Hill

Ls21-40_609428.indd 35   2/24/07 12:50:02 PM

LESSON 35 • SIDE 1

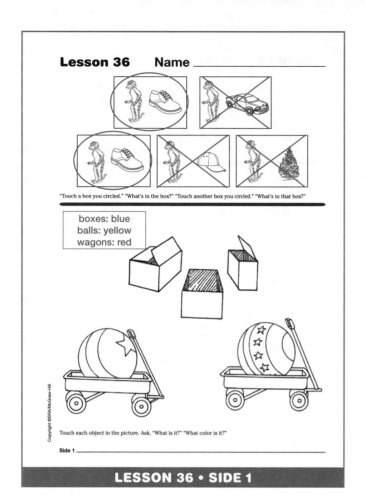

Lesson 36   Name _____

"Touch a box you circled." "What's in the box?" "Touch another box you circled." "What's in that box?"

boxes: blue
balls: yellow
wagons: red

Touch each object in the picture. Ask, "What is it?" "What color is it?"

Side 1 _____

LESSON 36 • SIDE 1

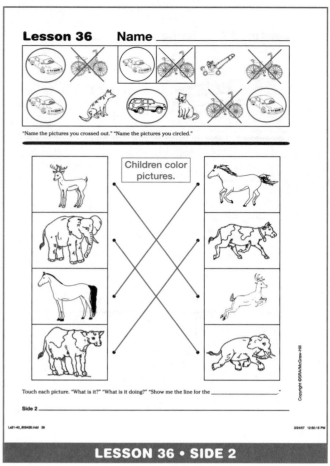

Lesson 36   Name _____

"Name the pictures you crossed out." "Name the pictures you circled."

Children color pictures.

Touch each picture. "What is it?" "What is it doing?" "Show me the line for the _____."

Side 2 _____

LESSON 36 • SIDE 2

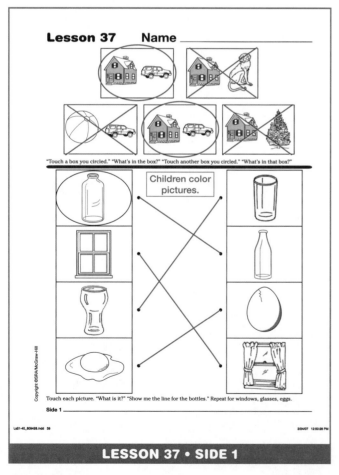

Lesson 37   Name _____

"Touch a box you circled." "What's in the box?" "Touch another box you circled." "What's in that box?"

Children color pictures.

Touch each picture. "What is it?" "Show me the line for the bottles." Repeat for windows, glasses, eggs.

Side 1 _____

LESSON 37 • SIDE 1

Lesson 37   Name _____

"Name the pictures you crossed out." "Name the pictures you circled."

cars: red
birds: blue
houses: yellow

Say, "Touch a house." "What color is it?" "Touch a bird." "What color is it?" "Touch a car." "What color is it?"

Side 2 _____

LESSON 37 • SIDE 2

10

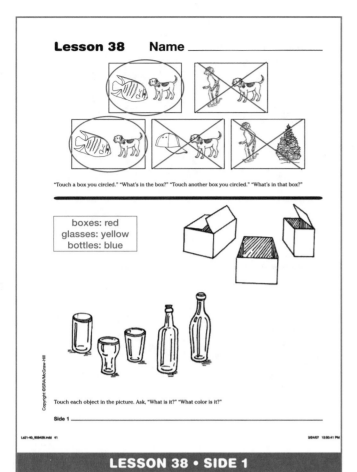

Lesson 38   Name _____

"Touch a box you circled." "What's in the box?" "Touch another box you circled." "What's in that box?"

boxes: red
glasses: yellow
bottles: blue

Touch each object in the picture. Ask, "What is it?" "What color is it?"

Side 1 _____

Ls21-40_609428.indd 41   2/24/07 12:50:41 PM

LESSON 38 • SIDE 1

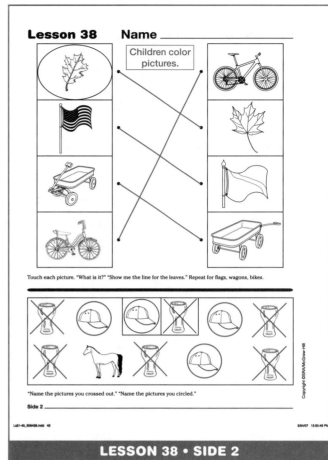

Lesson 38   Name _____

Children color pictures.

Touch each picture. "What is it?" "Show me the line for the leaves." Repeat for flags, wagons, bikes.

"Name the pictures you crossed out." "Name the pictures you circled."

Side 2 _____

Ls21-40_609428.indd 42   2/24/07 12:50:46 PM

LESSON 38 • SIDE 2

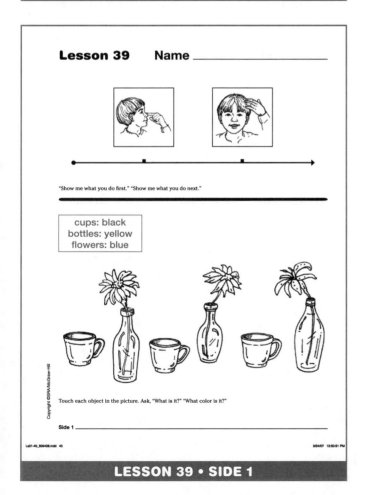

Lesson 39   Name _____

"Show me what you do first." "Show me what you do next."

cups: black
bottles: yellow
flowers: blue

Touch each object in the picture. Ask, "What is it?" "What color is it?"

Side 1 _____

Ls21-40_609428.indd 43   2/24/07 12:50:51 PM

LESSON 39 • SIDE 1

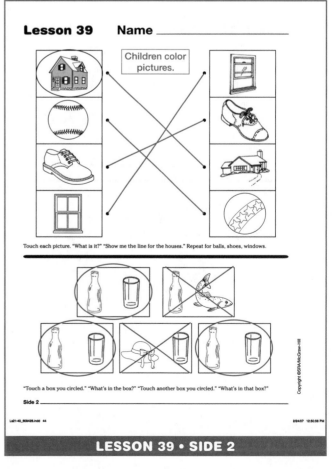

Lesson 39   Name _____

Children color pictures.

Touch each picture. "What is it?" "Show me the line for the houses." Repeat for balls, shoes, windows.

"Touch a box you circled." "What's in the box?" "Touch another box you circled." "What's in that box?"

Side 2 _____

Ls21-40_609428.indd 44   2/24/07 12:50:56 PM

LESSON 39 • SIDE 2

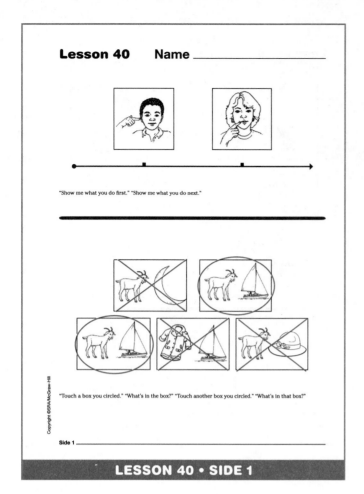

Lesson 40   Name _____

"Show me what you do first." "Show me what you do next."

"Touch a box you circled." "What's in the box?" "Touch another box you circled." "What's in that box?"

LESSON 40 • SIDE 1

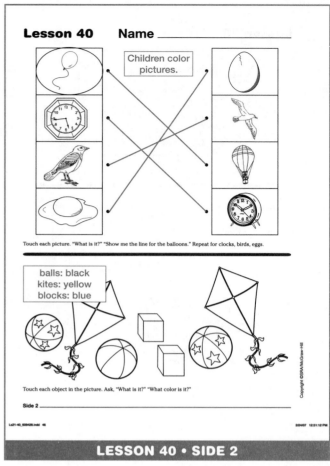

Lesson 40   Name _____

Children color pictures.

Touch each picture. "What is it?" "Show me the line for the balloons." Repeat for clocks, birds, eggs.

balls: black
kites: yellow
blocks: blue

Touch each object in the picture. Ask, "What is it?" "What color is it?"

LESSON 40 • SIDE 2

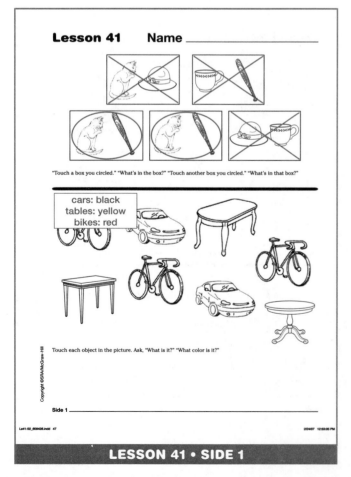

Lesson 41   Name _____

"Touch a box you circled." "What's in the box?" "Touch another box you circled." "What's in that box?"

cars: black
tables: yellow
bikes: red

Touch each object in the picture. Ask, "What is it?" "What color is it?"

LESSON 41 • SIDE 1

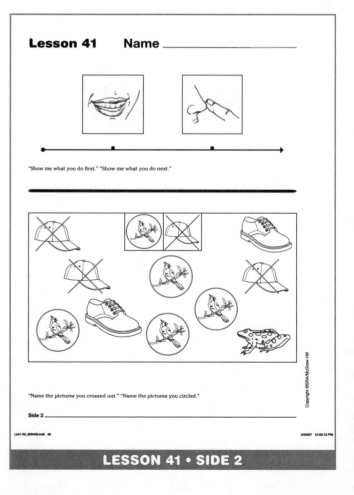

Lesson 41   Name _____

"Show me what you do first." "Show me what you do next."

"Name the pictures you crossed out." "Name the pictures you circled."

LESSON 41 • SIDE 2

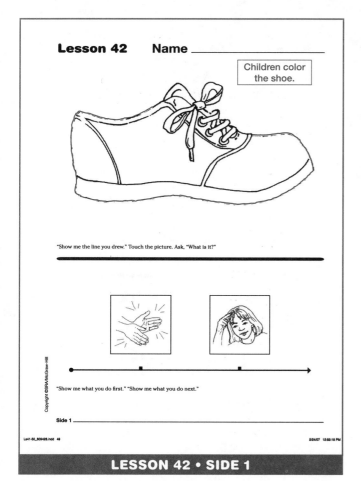

Lesson 42   Name _____

Children color
the shoe.

"Show me the line you drew." Touch the picture. Ask, "What is it?"

"Show me what you do first." "Show me what you do next."

Side 1 _____

LESSON 42 • SIDE 1

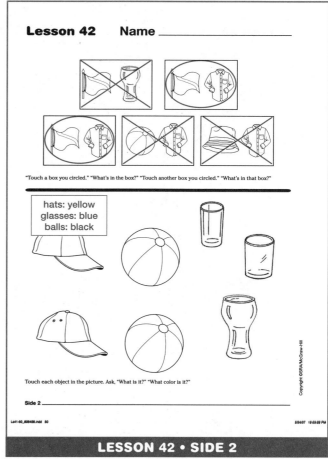

Lesson 42   Name _____

"Touch a box you circled." "What's in the box?" "Touch another box you circled." "What's in that box?"

hats: yellow
glasses: blue
balls: black

Touch each object in the picture. Ask, "What is it?" "What color is it?"

Side 2 _____

LESSON 42 • SIDE 2

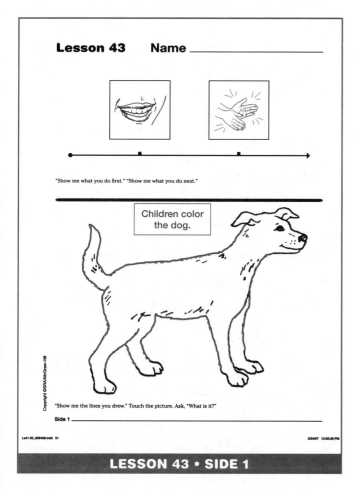

Lesson 43   Name _____

"Show me what you do first." "Show me what you do next."

Children color
the dog.

"Show me the lines you drew." Touch the picture. Ask, "What is it?"

Side 1 _____

LESSON 43 • SIDE 1

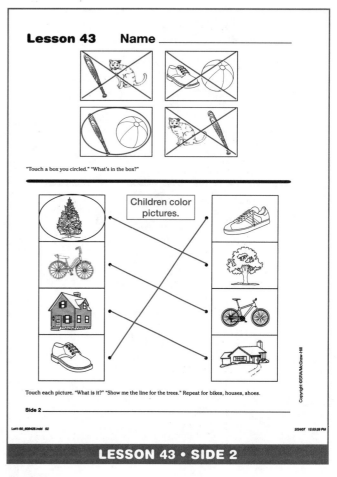

Lesson 43   Name _____

"Touch a box you circled." "What's in the box?"

Children color
pictures.

Touch each picture. "What is it?" "Show me the line for the trees." Repeat for bikes, houses, shoes.

Side 2 _____

LESSON 43 • SIDE 2

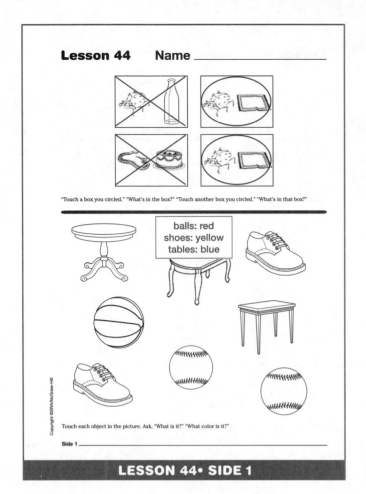

Lesson 44   Name _____

"Touch a box you circled." "What's in the box?" "Touch another box you circled." "What's in that box?"

balls: red
shoes: yellow
tables: blue

Touch each object in the picture. Ask, "What is it?" "What color is it?"

Side 1 _____

LESSON 44• SIDE 1

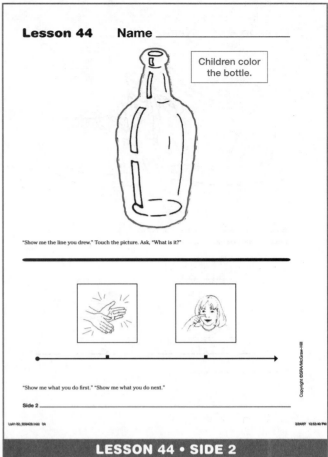

Lesson 44   Name _____

Children color
the bottle.

"Show me the line you drew." Touch the picture. Ask, "What is it?"

"Show me what you do first." "Show me what you do next."

Side 2 _____

LESSON 44 • SIDE 2

Lesson 45   Name _____

"Show me what you do first." "Show me what you do next."

Children color
the girl.

"Show me the lines you drew." Touch the picture. Ask, "What is it?"

Side 1 _____

LESSON 45 • SIDE 1

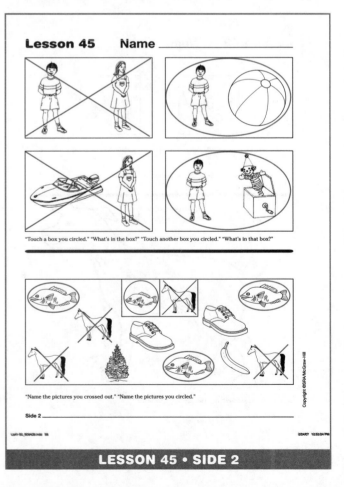

Lesson 45   Name _____

"Touch a box you circled." "What's in the box?" "Touch another box you circled." "What's in that box?"

"Name the pictures you crossed out." "Name the pictures you circled."

Side 2 _____

LESSON 45 • SIDE 2

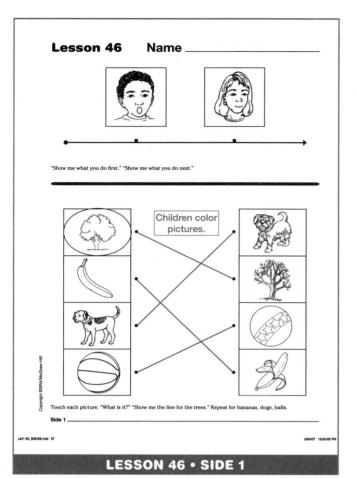

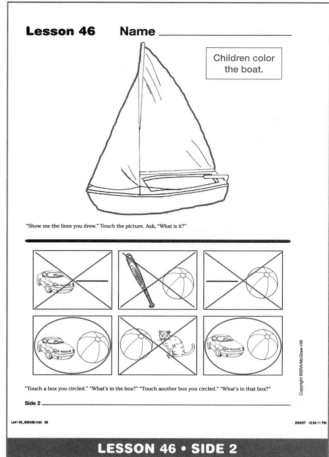

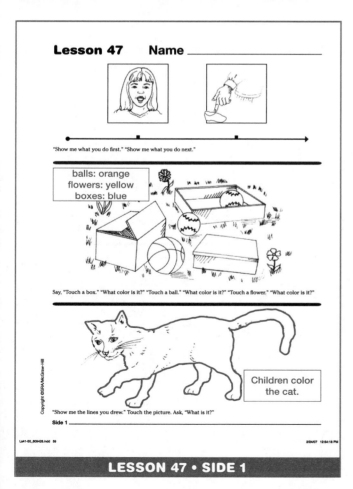

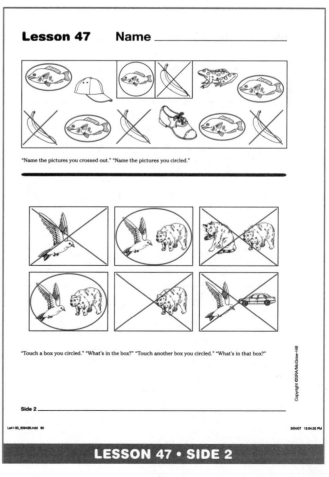

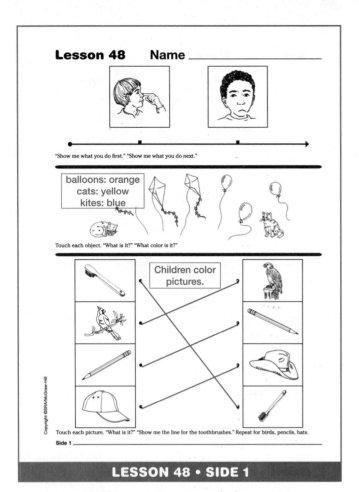

Lesson 48 Name _____

"Show me what you do first." "Show me what you do next."

balloons: orange
cats: yellow
kites: blue

Touch each object. "What is it?" "What color is it?"

Children color
pictures.

Touch each picture. "What is it?" "Show me the line for the toothbrushes." Repeat for birds, pencils, hats.

Side 1 _____

Copyright ©SRA/McGraw-Hill

LESSON 48 • SIDE 1

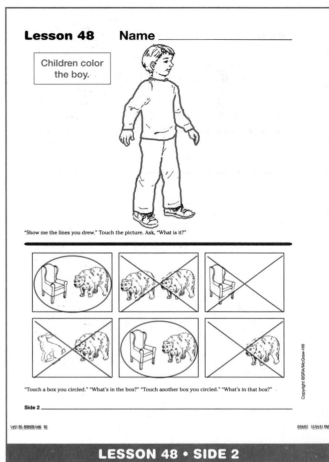

Lesson 48 Name _____

Children color
the boy.

"Show me the lines you drew." Touch the picture. Ask, "What is it?"

"Touch a box you circled." "What's in the box?" "Touch another box you circled." "What's in that box?"

Side 2 _____

Copyright ©SRA/McGraw-Hill

LESSON 48 • SIDE 2

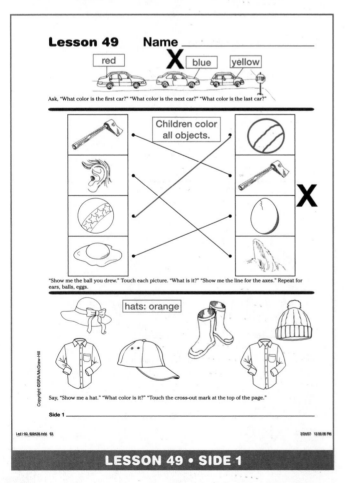

Lesson 49 Name _____

red   blue   yellow

Ask, "What color is the first car?" "What color is the next car?" "What color is the last car?"

Children color
all objects.

"Show me the ball you drew." Touch each picture. "What is it?" "Show me the line for the axes." Repeat for ears, balls, eggs.

hats: orange

Say, "Show me a hat." "What color is it?" "Touch the cross-out mark at the top of the page."

Side 1 _____

Copyright ©SRA/McGraw-Hill

LESSON 49 • SIDE 1

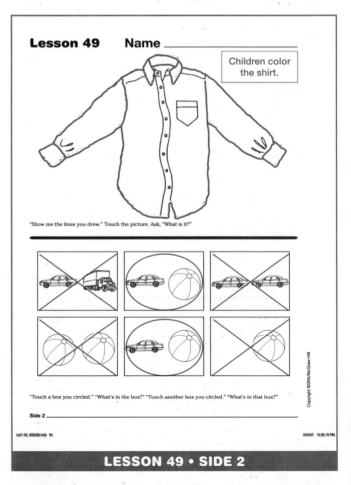

Lesson 49 Name _____

Children color
the shirt.

"Show me the lines you drew." Touch the picture. Ask, "What is it?"

"Touch a box you circled." "What's in the box?" "Touch another box you circled." "What's in that box?"

Side 2 _____

Copyright ©SRA/McGraw-Hill

LESSON 49 • SIDE 2

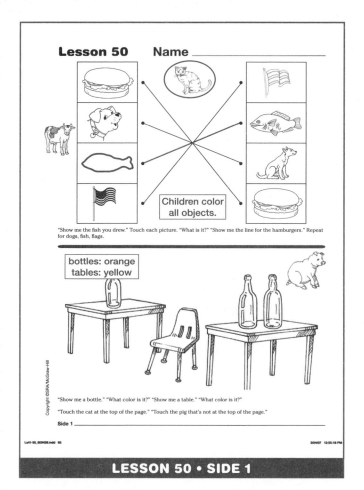

Lesson 50 Name _____

Children color all objects.

"Show me the fish you drew." Touch each picture. "What is it?" "Show me the line for the hamburgers." Repeat for dogs, fish, flags.

bottles: orange
tables: yellow

"Show me a bottle." "What color is it?" "Show me a table." "What color is it?"

"Touch the cat at the top of the page." "Touch the pig that's not at the top of the page."

Side 1 _____

LESSON 50 • SIDE 1

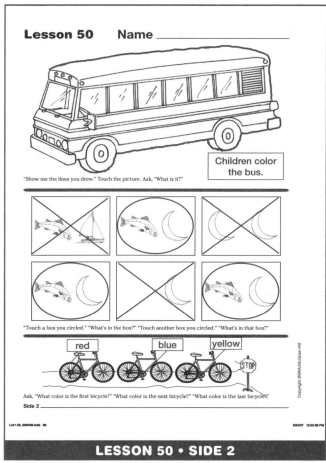

Lesson 50 Name _____

Children color the bus.

"Show me the lines you drew." Touch the picture. Ask, "What is it?"

"Touch a box you circled." "What's in the box?" "Touch another box you circled." "What's in that box?"

red   blue   yellow

Ask, "What color is the first bicycle?" "What color is the next bicycle?" "What color is the last bicycle?"

Side 2 _____

LESSON 50 • SIDE 2

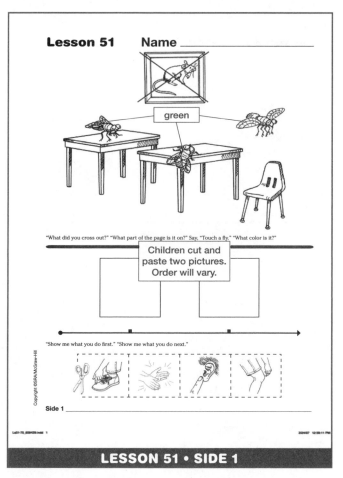

Lesson 51 Name _____

green

"What did you cross out?" "What part of the page is it on?" Say, "Touch a fly." "What color is it?"

Children cut and paste two pictures. Order will vary.

"Show me what you do first." "Show me what you do next."

Side 1 _____

LESSON 51 • SIDE 1

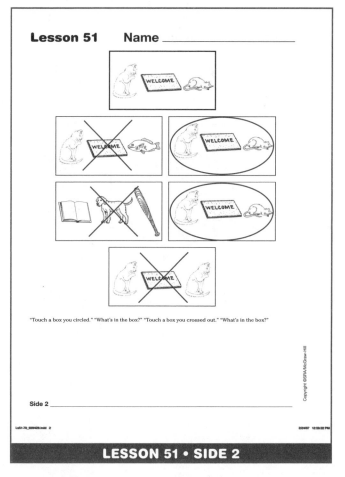

Lesson 51 Name _____

WELCOME

"Touch a box you circled." "What's in the box?" "Touch a box you crossed out." "What's in the box?"

Side 2 _____

LESSON 51 • SIDE 2

Lesson 52   Name _____

"Touch the animal that's first in line." "Touch the animal that's next in line."

yellow

yellow

green

red

Touch each object. Ask, "What is it?" "What color is it? "

"Show me the lines you drew." Touch the picture. Ask, "What is it?"

Children color shoe.

"Touch the mark at the top of the page." "Touch the mark at the bottom of the page."

Side 1 _____

LESSON 52 • SIDE 1

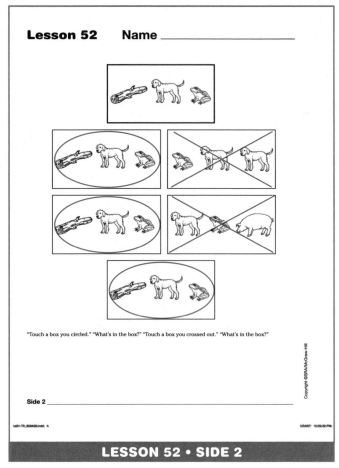

Lesson 52   Name _____

"Touch a box you circled." "What's in the box?" "Touch a box you crossed out." "What's in the box?"

Side 2 _____

Ls51-70_509442s.indd 4

2/24/07 12:59:30 PM

LESSON 52 • SIDE 2

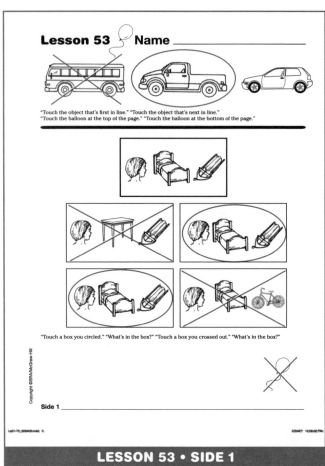

Lesson 53   Name _____

"Touch the object that's first in line." "Touch the object that's next in line."
"Touch the balloon at the top of the page." "Touch the balloon at the bottom of the page."

"Touch a box you circled." "What's in the box?" "Touch a box you crossed out." "What's in the box?"

Side 1 _____

Ls51-70_509442s.indd 5

2/24/07 12:59:32 PM

LESSON 53 • SIDE 1

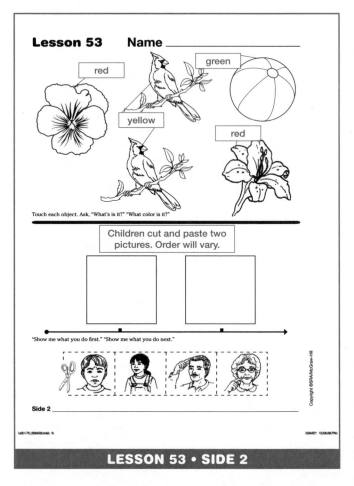

Lesson 53   Name _____

red

green

yellow

red

Touch each object. Ask, "What's is it?" "What color is it?"

Children cut and paste two pictures. Order will vary.

"Show me what you do first." "Show me what you do next."

Side 2 _____

Ls51-70_509442s.indd 6

2/24/07 12:59:36 PM

LESSON 53 • SIDE 2

18

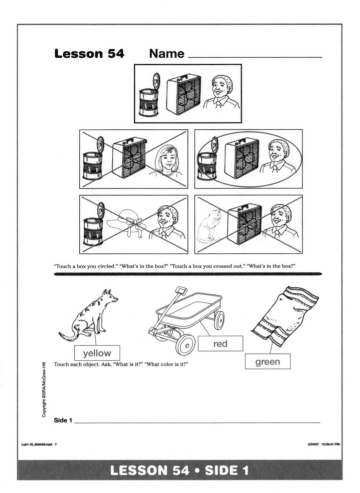

Lesson 54   Name _____

"Touch a box you circled." "What's in the box?" "Touch a box you crossed out." "What's in the box?"

yellow   red   green

Touch each object. Ask, "What is it?" "What color is it?"

Side 1 _____

LESSON 54 • SIDE 1

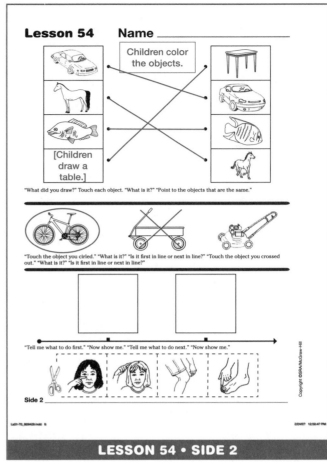

Lesson 54   Name _____

Children color the objects.

[Children draw a table.]

"What did you draw?" Touch each object. "What is it?" "Point to the objects that are the same."

"Touch the object you cirled." "What is it?" "Is it first in line or next in line?" "Touch the object you crossed out." "What is it?" "Is it first in line or next in line?"

"Tell me what to do first." "Now show me." "Tell me what to do next." "Now show me."

Side 2 _____

LESSON 54 • SIDE 2

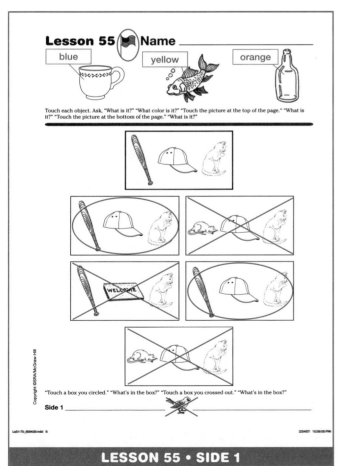

Lesson 55   Name _____

blue   yellow   orange

Touch each object. Ask, "What is it?" "What color is it?" "Touch the picture at the top of the page." "What is it?" "Touch the picture at the bottom of the page." "What is it?"

WELCOME

"Touch a box you circled." "What's in the box?" "Touch a box you crossed out." "What's in the box?"

Side 1 _____

LESSON 55 • SIDE 1

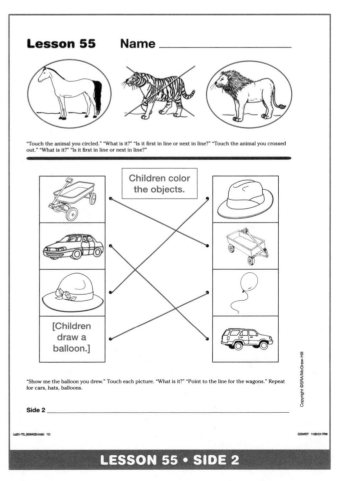

Lesson 55   Name _____

"Touch the animal you circled." "What is it?" "Is it first in line or next in line?" "Touch the animal you crossed out." "What is it?" "Is it first in line or next in line?"

Children color the objects.

[Children draw a balloon.]

"Show me the balloon you drew." Touch each picture. "What is it?" "Point to the line for the wagons." Repeat for cars, hats, balloons.

Side 2 _____

LESSON 55 • SIDE 2

Lesson 56 ~~X~~ Name _____

orange

green

red

Touch each object. Ask, "What is it?" "What color is it?"

Children color
the table.

Touch the picture. "What is it?" "Show me the line you drew." "What part of the table did you draw?" "Tell me
the parts of the table."

"Touch the hamburger." "Is it at the top or the bottom of the page?" "Touch the elephant." "Is it at the top or
the bottom of the page?"
Side 1 _____

LESSON 56 • SIDE 1

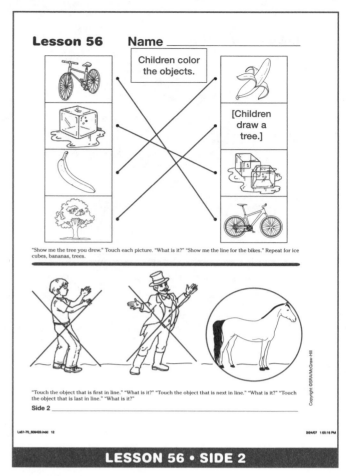

Lesson 56   Name _____

Children color
the objects.

[Children
draw a
tree.]

"Show me the tree you drew." Touch each picture. "What is it?" "Show me the line for the bikes." Repeat for ice
cubes, bananas, trees.

"Touch the object that is first in line." "What is it?" "Touch the object that is next in line." "What is it?" "Touch
the object that is last in line." "What is it?"
Side 2 _____

Ls51-70_608420.indd 12   2/24/07 1:00:16 PM

LESSON 56 • SIDE 2

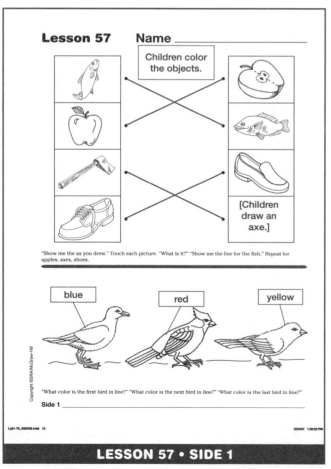

Lesson 57   Name _____

Children color
the objects.

[Children
draw an
axe.]

"Show me the ax you drew." Touch each picture. "What is it?" "Show me the line for the fish." Repeat for
apples, axes, shoes.

blue

red

yellow

"What color is the first bird in line?" "What color is the next bird in line?" "What color is the last bird in line?"
Side 1 _____

Ls51-70_608420.indd 13   2/24/07 1:00:23 PM

LESSON 57 • SIDE 1

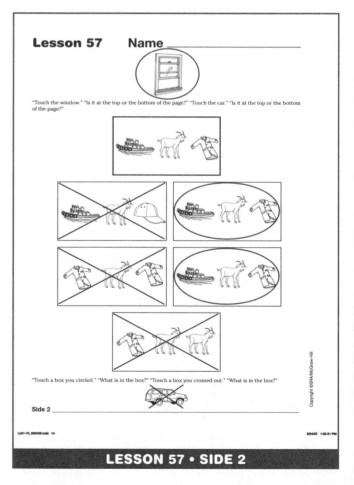

Lesson 57   Name _____

"Touch the window." "Is it at the top or the bottom of the page?" "Touch the car." "Is it at the top or the bottom
of the page?"

"Touch a box you circled." "What is in the box?" "Touch a box you crossed out." "What is in the box?"

Side 2 _____

Ls51-70_608420.indd 14   2/24/07 1:00:31 PM

LESSON 57 • SIDE 2

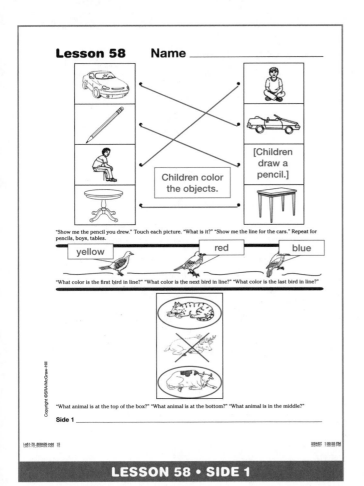

Lesson 58 Name _____

Children color the objects.

[Children draw a pencil.]

"Show me the pencil you drew." Touch each picture. "What is it?" "Show me the line for the cars." Repeat for pencils, boys, tables.

yellow red blue

"What color is the first bird in line?" "What color is the next bird in line?" "What color is the last bird in line?"

"What animal is at the top of the box?" "What animal is at the bottom?" "What animal is in the middle?"

Side 1 _____

LESSON 58 • SIDE 1

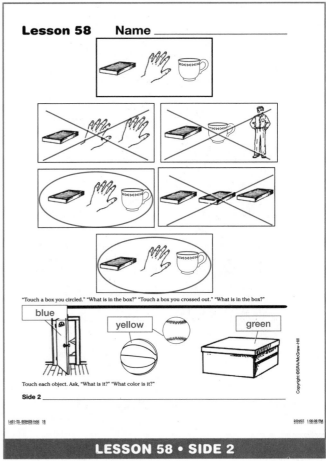

Lesson 58 Name _____

"Touch a box you circled." "What is in the box?" "Touch a box you crossed out." "What is in the box?"

blue yellow green

Touch each object. Ask, "What is it?" "What color is it?"

Side 2 _____

LESSON 58 • SIDE 2

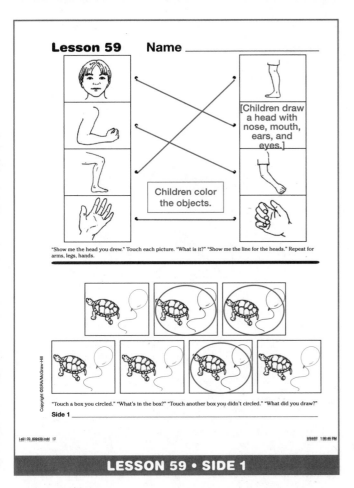

Lesson 59 Name _____

Children color the objects.

[Children draw a head with nose, mouth, ears, and eyes.]

"Show me the head you drew." Touch each picture. "What is it?" "Show me the line for the heads." Repeat for arms, legs, hands.

"Touch a box you circled." "What's in the box?" "Touch another box you didn't circled." "What did you draw?"

Side 1 _____

LESSON 59 • SIDE 1

Lesson 59 Name _____

"Touch the picture you circled." "What is it?" "Is it first in line or next in line?" "Touch the picture you crossed out." "What is it?" "Is it first in line or next in line?"

"What animal is at the top of the box?" "What animal is at the bottom?" "What animal is in the middle?"

Side 2 _____

LESSON 59 • SIDE 2

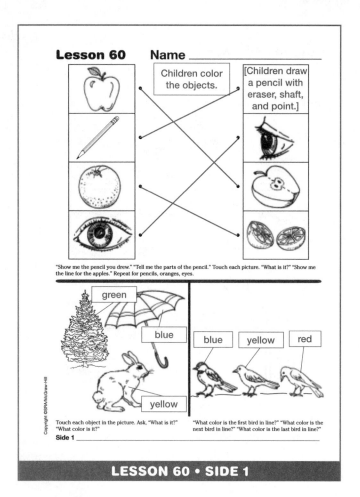

Lesson 60 Name _____

Children color the objects.

[Children draw a pencil with eraser, shaft, and point.]

"Show me the pencil you drew." "Tell me the parts of the pencil." Touch each picture. "What is it?" "Show me the line for the apples." Repeat for pencils, oranges, eyes.

green

blue

blue   yellow   red

yellow

Touch each object in the picture. Ask, "What is it?" "What color is it?"

"What color is the first bird in line?" "What color is the next bird in line?" "What color is the last bird in line?"

Side 1 _____

LESSON 60 • SIDE 1

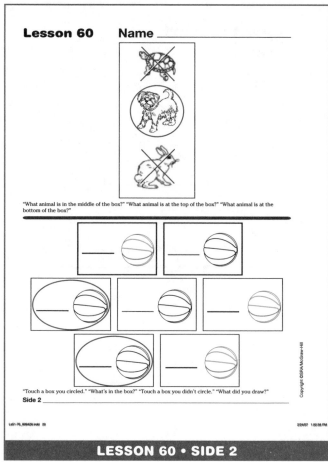

Lesson 60 Name _____

"What animal is in the middle of the box?" "What animal is at the top of the box?" "What animal is at the bottom of the box?"

"Touch a box you circled." "What's in the box?" "Touch a box you didn't circle." "What did you draw?"

Side 2 _____

LESSON 60 • SIDE 2

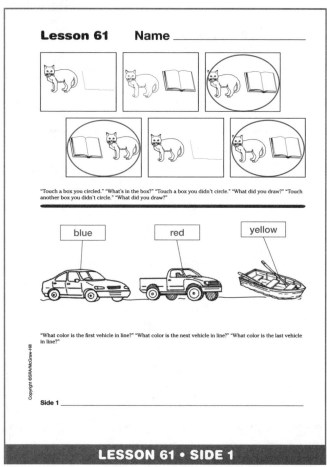

Lesson 61 Name _____

"Touch a box you circled." "What's in the box?" "Touch a box you didn't circle." "What did you draw?" "Touch another box you didn't circle." "What did you draw?"

blue   red   yellow

"What color is the first vehicle in line?" "What color is the next vehicle in line?" "What color is the last vehicle in line?"

Side 1 _____

LESSON 61 • SIDE 1

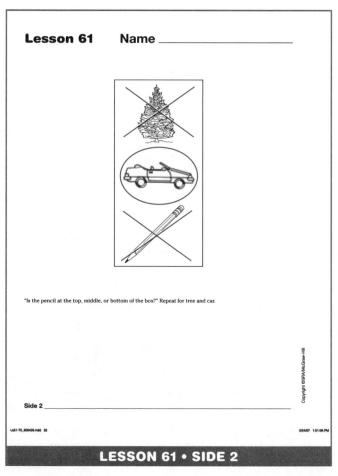

Lesson 61 Name _____

"Is the pencil at the top, middle, or bottom of the box?" Repeat for tree and car.

Side 2 _____

LESSON 61 • SIDE 2

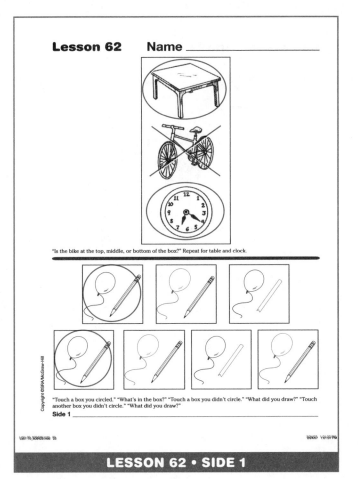

Lesson 62 Name _____

"Is the bike at the top, middle, or bottom of the box?" Repeat for table and clock.

"Touch a box you circled." "What's in the box?" "Touch a box you didn't circle." "What did you draw?" "Touch another box you didn't circle." "What did you draw?"

Side 1 _____

LESSON 62 • SIDE 1

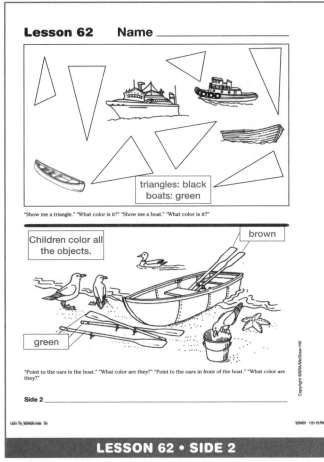

Lesson 62 Name _____

triangles: black
boats: green

"Show me a triangle." "What color is it?" "Show me a boat." "What color is it?"

Children color all the objects.

brown

green

"Point to the oars in the boat." "What color are they?" "Point to the oars in front of the boat." "What color are they?"

Side 2 _____

LESSON 62 • SIDE 2

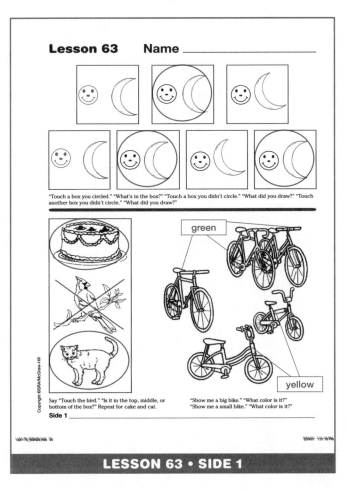

Lesson 63 Name _____

"Touch a box you circled." "What's in the box?" "Touch a box you didn't circle." "What did you draw?" "Touch another box you didn't circle." "What did you draw?"

green

yellow

Say "Touch the bird." "Is it in the top, middle, or bottom of the box?" Repeat for cake and cat.

"Show me a big bike." "What color is it?" "Show me a small bike." "What color is it?"

Side 1 _____

LESSON 63 • SIDE 1

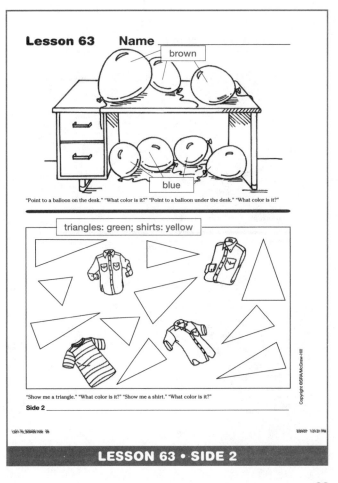

Lesson 63 Name _____

brown

blue

"Point to a balloon on the desk." "What color is it?" "Point to a balloon under the desk." "What color is it?"

triangles: green; shirts: yellow

"Show me a triangle." "What color is it?" "Show me a shirt." "What color is it?"

Side 2 _____

LESSON 63 • SIDE 2

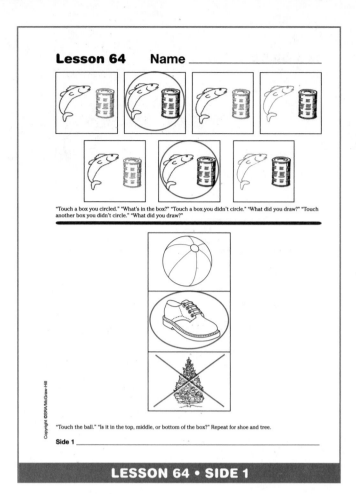

Lesson 64   Name _____

"Touch a box you circled." "What's in the box?" "Touch a box you didn't circle." "What did you draw?" "Touch another box you didn't circle." "What did you draw?"

"Touch the ball." "Is it in the top, middle, or bottom of the box?" Repeat for shoe and tree.

Side 1 _____

LESSON 64 • SIDE 1

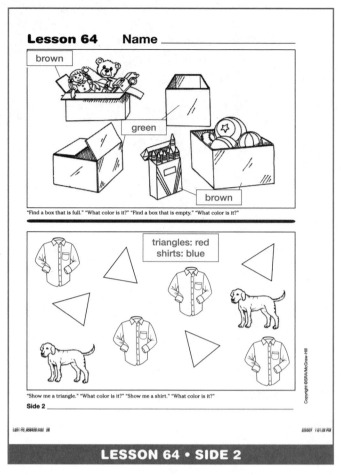

Lesson 64   Name _____

brown

green

brown

"Find a box that is full." "What color is it?" "Find a box that is empty." "What color is it?"

triangles: red
shirts: blue

"Show me a triangle." "What color is it?" "Show me a shirt." "What color is it?"

Side 2 _____

LESSON 64 • SIDE 2

Lesson 65   Name _____

buckets: green
boats: brown
oars: yellow

"Show me a bucket." "What color is it?" Repeat for boat and oar.

blue

green

"Show me a big flag." "What color is it?" "Show me a small flag." "What color is it?"

Side 1 _____

LESSON 65 • SIDE 1

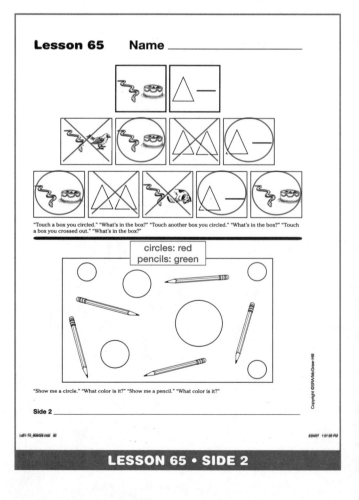

Lesson 65   Name _____

"Touch a box you circled." "What's in the box?" "Touch another box you circled." "What's in the box?" "Touch a box you crossed out." "What's in the box?"

circles: red
pencils: green

"Show me a circle." "What color is it?" "Show me a pencil." "What color is it?"

Side 2 _____

LESSON 65 • SIDE 2

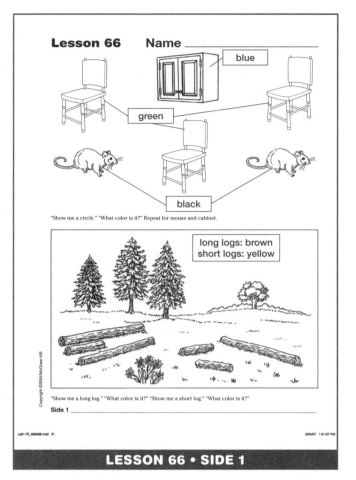

Lesson 66   Name _____

blue

green

black

"Show me a circle." "What color is it?" Repeat for mouse and cabinet.

long logs: brown
short logs: yellow

"Show me a long log." "What color is it?" "Show me a short log." "What color is it?"

Side 1 _____

La51-70_609429.indd 31   2/24/07 1:01:57 PM

LESSON 66 • SIDE 1

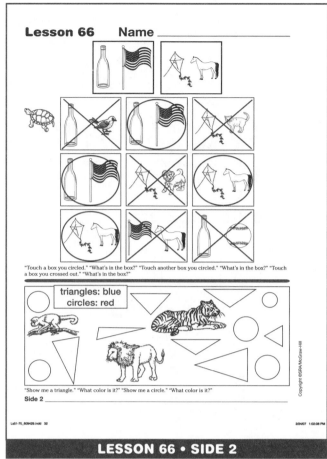

Lesson 66   Name _____

"Touch a box you circled." "What's in the box?" "Touch another box you circled." "What's in the box?" "Touch a box you crossed out." "What's in the box?"

triangles: blue
circles: red

"Show me a triangle." "What color is it?" "Show me a circle." "What color is it?"

Side 2 _____

La51-70_609429.indd 32   2/24/07 1:02:08 PM

LESSON 66 • SIDE 2

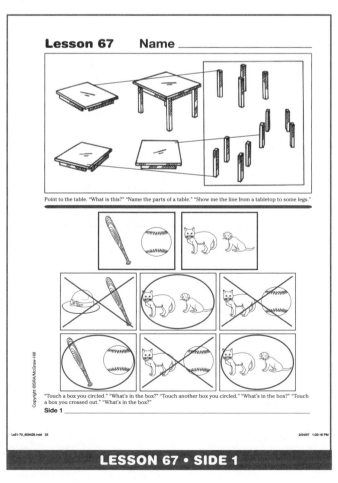

Lesson 67   Name _____

"Point to the table." "What is this?" "Name the parts of a table." "Show me the line from a tabletop to some legs."

"Touch a box you circled." "What's in the box?" "Touch another box you circled." "What's in the box?" "Touch a box you crossed out." "What's in the box?"

Side 1 _____

La51-70_609429.indd 33   2/24/07 1:02:16 PM

LESSON 67 • SIDE 1

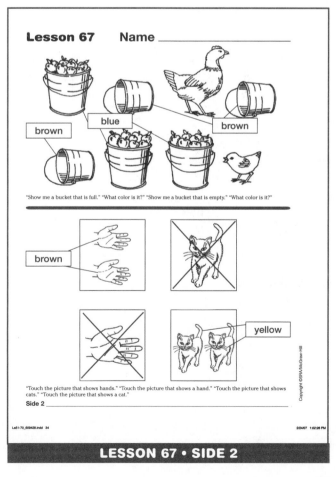

Lesson 67   Name _____

brown   blue   brown

"Show me a bucket that is full." "What color is it?" "Show me a bucket that is empty." "What color is it?"

brown

yellow

"Touch the picture that shows hands." "Touch the picture that shows a hand." "Touch the picture that shows cats." "Touch the picture that shows a cat."

Side 2 _____

La51-70_609429.indd 34   2/24/07 1:02:28 PM

LESSON 67 • SIDE 2

Lesson 68   Name _____

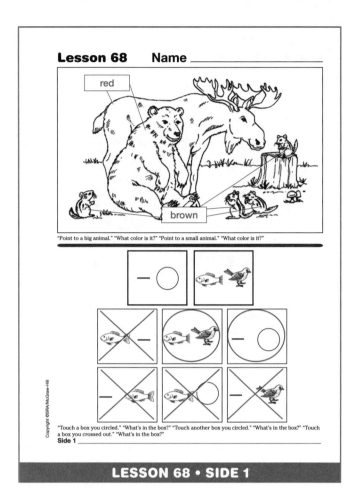

"Point to a big animal." "What color is it?" "Point to a small animal." "What color is it?"

"Touch a box you circled." "What's in the box?" "Touch another box you circled." "What's in the box?" "Touch a box you crossed out." "What's in the box?"
Side 1 _____

LESSON 68 • SIDE 1

Lesson 68   Name _____

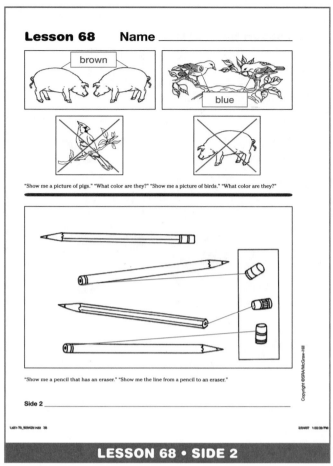

"Show me a picture of pigs." "What color are they?" "Show me a picture of birds." "What color are they?"

"Show me a pencil that has an eraser." "Show me the line from a pencil to an eraser."

Side 2 _____

LESSON 68 • SIDE 2

Lesson 69   Name _____

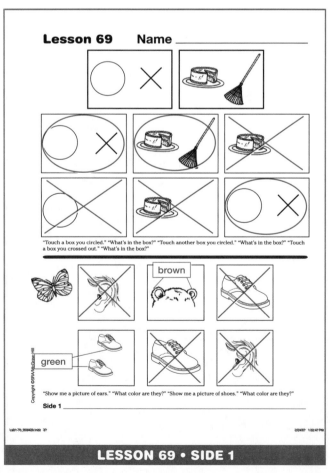

"Touch a box you circled." "What's in the box?" "Touch another box you circled." "What's in the box?" "Touch a box you crossed out." "What's in the box?"

"Show me a picture of ears." "What color are they?" "Show me a picture of shoes." "What color are they?"
Side 1 _____

LESSON 69 • SIDE 1

Lesson 69   Name _____

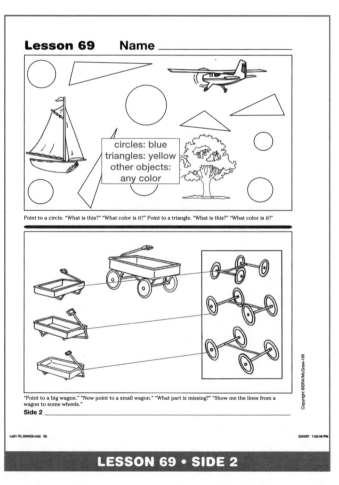

Point to a circle. "What is this?" "What color is it?" Point to a triangle. "What is this?" "What color is it?"

"Point to a big wagon." "Now point to a small wagon." "What part is missing?" "Show me the lines from a wagon to some wheels."
Side 2 _____

LESSON 69 • SIDE 2

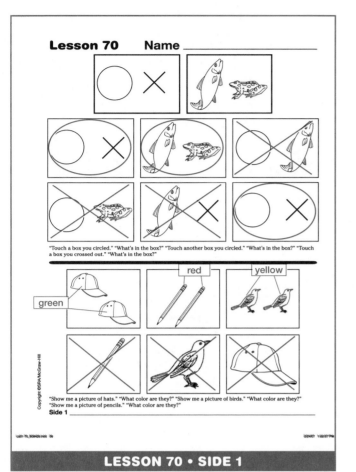

Lesson 70   Name _____

"Touch a box you circled." "What's in the box?" "Touch another box you circled." "What's in the box?" "Touch a box you crossed out." "What's in the box?"

green   red   yellow

"Show me a picture of hats." "What color are they?" "Show me a picture of birds." "What color are they?"
"Show me a picture of pencils." "What color are they?"
Side 1 _____

LESSON 70 • SIDE 1

Lesson 70   Name _____

circles: green
triangles: yellow
other objects:
any color

Point to a circle. "What is this?" "What color is it?" Point to a triangle. "What is this?" "What color is it?"

boxes: blue
cats: yellow
squirrels: black

"Show me a cat." "What color is it?" "Show me a box." "What color is it?" "Show me a squirrel."
"What color is it?"
Side 2 _____

LESSON 70 • SIDE 2

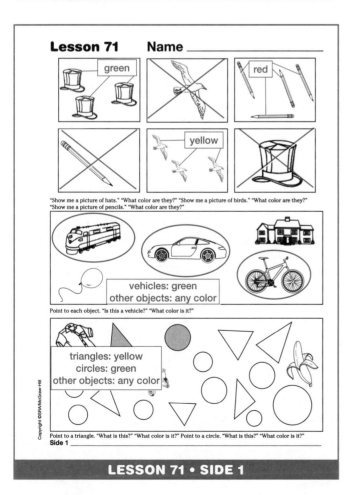

Lesson 71   Name _____

green   red   yellow

"Show me a picture of hats." "What color are they?" "Show me a picture of birds." "What color are they?"
"Show me a picture of pencils." "What color are they?"

vehicles: green
other objects: any color

Point to each object. "Is this a vehicle?" "What color is it?"

triangles: yellow
circles: green
other objects: any color

Point to a triangle. "What is this?" "What color is it?" Point to a circle. "What is this?" "What color is it?"
Side 1 _____

LESSON 71 • SIDE 1

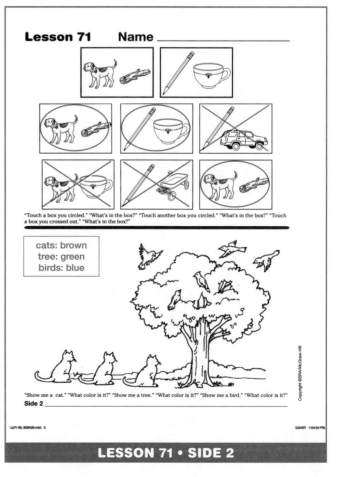

Lesson 71   Name _____

"Touch a box you circled." "What's in the box?" "Touch another box you circled." "What's in the box?" "Touch a box you crossed out." "What's in the box?"

cats: brown
tree: green
birds: blue

"Show me a cat." "What color is it?" "Show me a tree." "What color is it?" "Show me a bird." "What color is it?"
Side 2 _____

LESSON 71 • SIDE 2

27

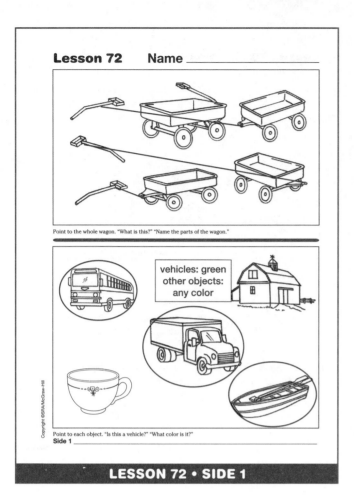

Lesson 72   Name _____

Point to the whole wagon. "What is this?" "Name the parts of the wagon."

vehicles: green
other objects:
any color

Point to each object. "Is this a vehicle?" "What color is it?"
Side 1

LESSON 72 • SIDE 1

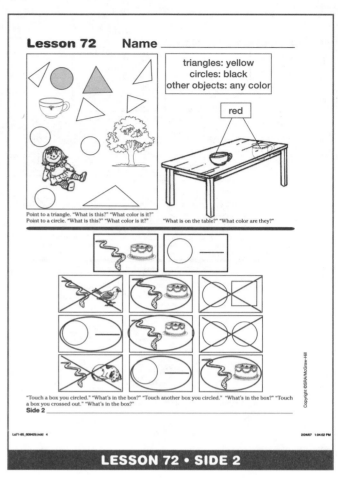

Lesson 72   Name _____

triangles: yellow
circles: black
other objects: any color

red

Point to a triangle. "What is this?" "What color is it?"
Point to a circle. "What is this?" "What color is it?"

"What is on the table?" "What color are they?"

"Touch a box you circled." "What's in the box?" "Touch another box you circled." "What's in the box?" "Touch a box you crossed out." "What's in the box?"
Side 2

Ls71-85_609429.indd 4   2/24/07 1:04:52 PM

LESSON 72 • SIDE 2

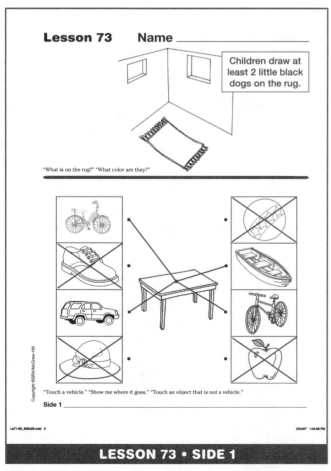

Lesson 73   Name _____

Children draw at
least 2 little black
dogs on the rug.

"What is on the rug?" "What color are they?"

"Touch a vehicle." "Show me where it goes." "Touch an object that is not a vehicle."

Side 1

Ls71-85_609429.indd 5   2/24/07 1:04:58 PM

LESSON 73 • SIDE 1

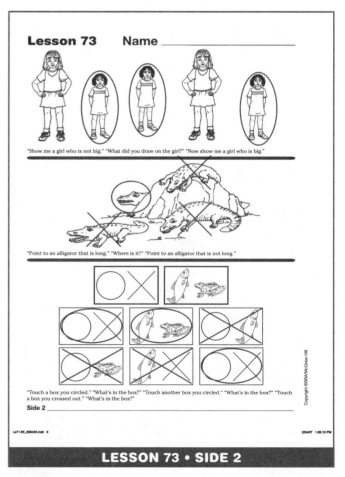

Lesson 73   Name _____

"Show me a girl who is not big." "What did you draw on the girl?" "Now show me a girl who is big."

"Point to an alligator that is long." "Where is it?" "Point to an alligator that is not long."

"Touch a box you circled." "What's in the box?" "Touch another box you circled." "What's in the box?" "Touch a box you crossed out." "What's in the box?"
Side 2

Ls71-85_609429.indd 6   2/24/07 1:05:10 PM

LESSON 73 • SIDE 2

28

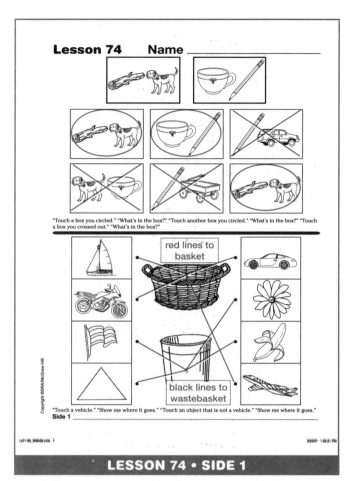

Lesson 74   Name _____

"Touch a box you circled." "What's in the box?" "Touch another box you circled." "What's in the box?" "Touch a box you crossed out." "What's in the box?"

red lines to basket

black lines to wastebasket

"Touch a vehicle." "Show me where it goes." "Touch an object that is not a vehicle." "Show me where it goes."

Side 1 _____

LESSON 74 • SIDE 1

Lesson 74   Name _____

Children add water drops.

"Show me a girl who is wet." "What did you draw on the girl?" "Show me a girl who is not wet."

triangles: blue circles: orange other objects: any color

Point to a triangle. "What is this?" "What color is it?" Point to a circle. "What is this?" "What color is it?"

Side 2 _____

LESSON 74 • SIDE 2

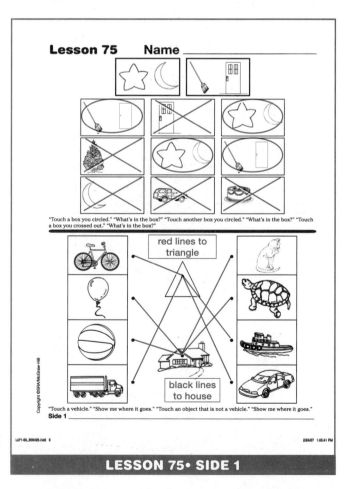

Lesson 75   Name _____

"Touch a box you circled." "What's in the box?" "Touch another box you circled." "What's in the box?" "Touch a box you crossed out." "What's in the box?"

red lines to triangle

black lines to house

"Touch a vehicle." "Show me where it goes." "Touch an object that is not a vehicle." "Show me where it goes."

Side 1 _____

LESSON 75• SIDE 1

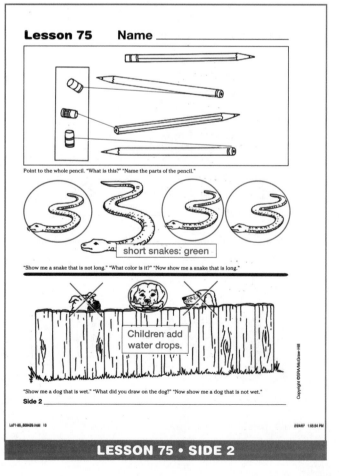

Lesson 75   Name _____

Point to the whole pencil. "What is this?" "Name the parts of the pencil."

short snakes: green

"Show me a snake that is not long." "What color is it?" "Now show me a snake that is long."

Children add water drops.

"Show me a dog that is wet." "What did you draw on the dog?" "Now show me a dog that is not wet."

Side 2 _____

LESSON 75 • SIDE 2

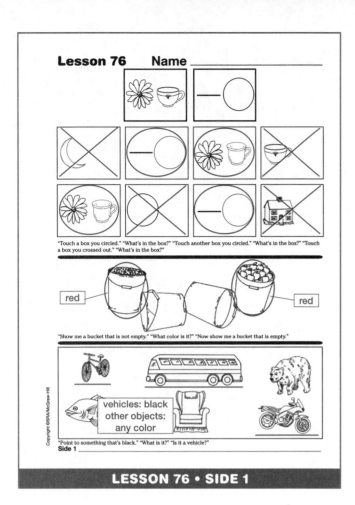

Lesson 76   Name _____

"Touch a box you circled." "What's in the box?" "Touch another box you circled." "What's in the box?" "Touch a box you crossed out." "What's in the box?"

red   red

"Show me a bucket that is not empty." "What color is it?" "Now show me a bucket that is empty."

vehicles: black
other objects:
any color

"Point to something that's black." "What is it?" "Is it a vehicle?"
Side 1 _____

LESSON 76 • SIDE 1

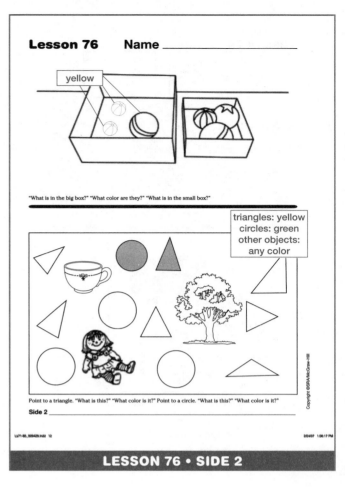

Lesson 76   Name _____

yellow

"What is in the big box?" "What color are they?" "What is in the small box?"

triangles: yellow
circles: green
other objects:
any color

Point to a triangle. "What is this?" "What color is it?" Point to a circle. "What is this?" "What color is it?"
Side 2 _____

LESSON 76 • SIDE 2

Lesson 77   Name _____

"Touch a box you circled." "What's in the box?" "Touch another box you circled." "What's in the box?" "Touch a box you crossed out." "What's in the box?"

"Show me a black cat." "What is it doing?"
Side 1 _____

LESSON 77 • SIDE 1

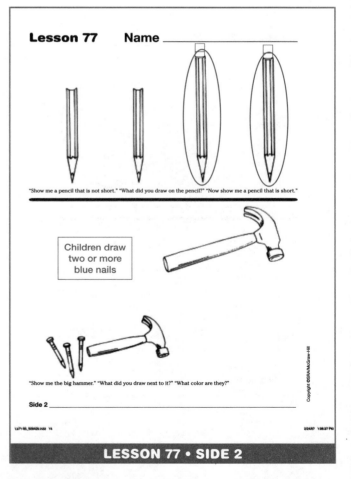

Lesson 77   Name _____

"Show me a pencil that is not short." "What did you draw on the pencil?" "Now show me a pencil that is short."

Children draw
two or more
blue nails

"Show me the big hammer." "What did you draw next to it?" "What color are they?"
Side 2 _____

LESSON 77 • SIDE 2

30

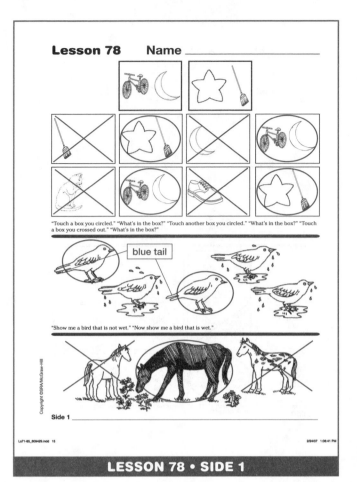

Lesson 78   Name _____

"Touch a box you circled." "What's in the box?" "Touch another box you circled." "What's in the box?" "Touch a box you crossed out." "What's in the box?"

blue tail

"Show me a bird that is not wet." "Now show me a bird that is wet."

Side 1 _____

Ls71-85_509429.indd 15   2/24/07 1:06:41 PM

LESSON 78 • SIDE 1

Lesson 78   Name _____

vehicles: green
other objects:
any color

Point to an object that is green. "Is this a vehicle?" "What is it called?" Repeat for another green object.

triangles: blue
circles: yellow
other objects:
any color

Point to a circle. "What is this?" "What color is it?" Point to a triangle. "What is this?" "What color is it?"

Side 2 _____

Ls71-85_509429.indd 16   2/24/07 1:06:51 PM

LESSON 78 • SIDE 2

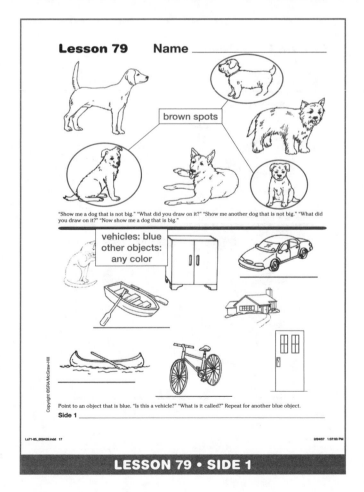

Lesson 79   Name _____

brown spots

"Show me a dog that is not big." "What did you draw on it?" "Show me another dog that is not big." "What did you draw on it?" "Now show me a dog that is big."

vehicles: blue
other objects:
any color

Point to an object that is blue. "Is this a vehicle?" "What is it called?" Repeat for another blue object.

Side 1 _____

Ls71-85_509429.indd 17   2/24/07 1:07:00 PM

LESSON 79 • SIDE 1

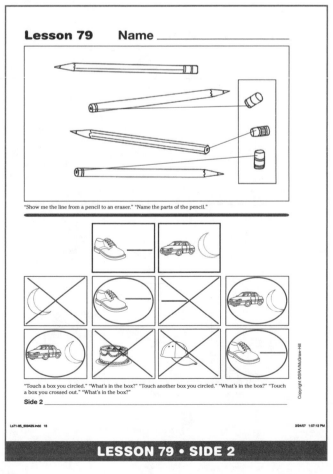

Lesson 79   Name _____

"Show me the line from a pencil to an eraser." "Name the parts of the pencil."

"Touch a box you circled." "What's in the box?" "Touch another box you circled." "What's in the box?" "Touch a box you crossed out." "What's in the box?"

Side 2 _____

Ls71-85_509429.indd 18   2/24/07 1:07:12 PM

LESSON 79 • SIDE 2

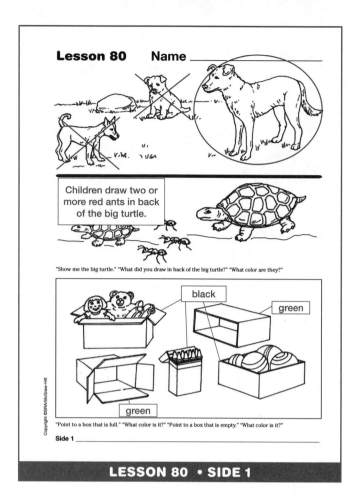

Lesson 80   Name _____

Children draw two or more red ants in back of the big turtle.

"Show me the big turtle." "What did you draw in back of the big turtle?" "What color are they?"

black

green

green

"Point to a box that is full." "What color is it?" "Point to a box that is empty." "What color is it?"

Side 1 _____

LESSON 80 • SIDE 1

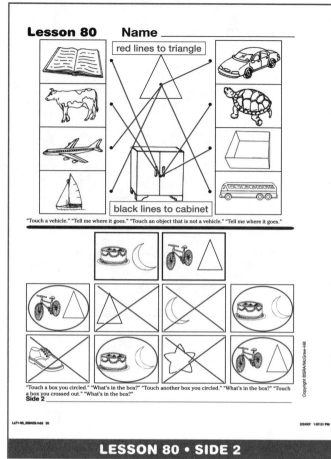

Lesson 80   Name _____

red lines to triangle

black lines to cabinet

"Touch a vehicle." "Tell me where it goes." "Touch an object that is not a vehicle." "Tell me where it goes."

"Touch a box you circled." "What's in the box?" "Touch another box you circled." "What's in the box?" "Touch a box you crossed out." "What's in the box?"

Side 2

LESSON 80 • SIDE 2

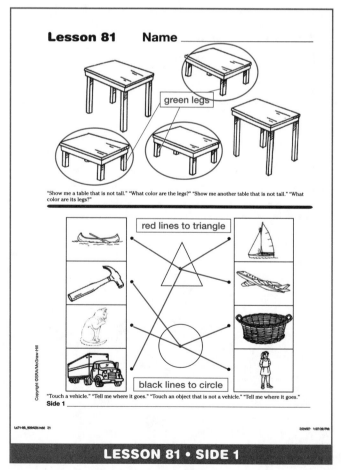

Lesson 81   Name _____

green legs

"Show me a table that is not tall." "What color are the legs?" "Show me another table that is not tall." "What color are its legs?"

red lines to triangle

black lines to circle

"Touch a vehicle." "Tell me where it goes." "Touch an object that is not a vehicle." "Tell me where it goes."

Side 1 _____

LESSON 81 • SIDE 1

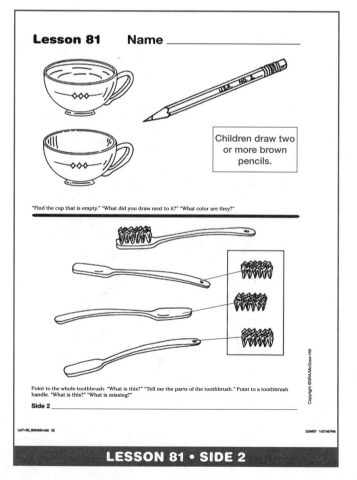

Lesson 81   Name _____

Children draw two or more brown pencils.

"Find the cup that is empty." "What did you draw next to it?" "What color are they?"

Point to the whole toothbrush. "What is this?" "Tell me the parts of the toothbrush." Point to a toothbrush handle. "What is this?" "What is missing?"

Side 2 _____

LESSON 81 • SIDE 2

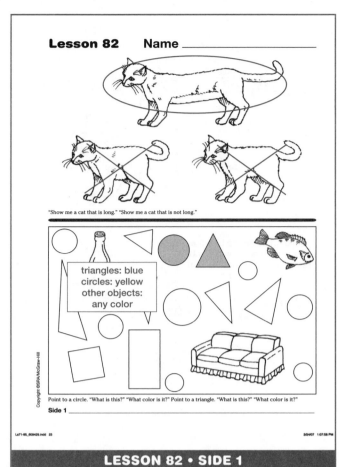

Lesson 82   Name _____

"Show me a cat that is long." "Show me a cat that is not long."

triangles: blue
circles: yellow
other objects:
  any color

Point to a circle. "What is this?" "What color is it?" Point to a triangle. "What is this?" "What color is it?"

Side 1 _____

LESSON 82 • SIDE 1

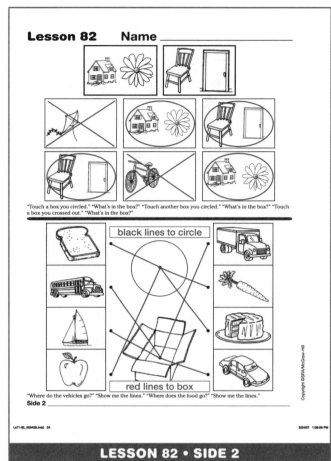

Lesson 82   Name _____

"Touch a box you circled." "What's in the box?" "Touch another box you circled." "What's in the box?" "Touch a box you crossed out." "What's in the box?"

black lines to circle

red lines to box

"Where do the vehicles go?" "Show me the lines." "Where does the food go?" "Show me the lines."

Side 2 _____

LESSON 82 • SIDE 2

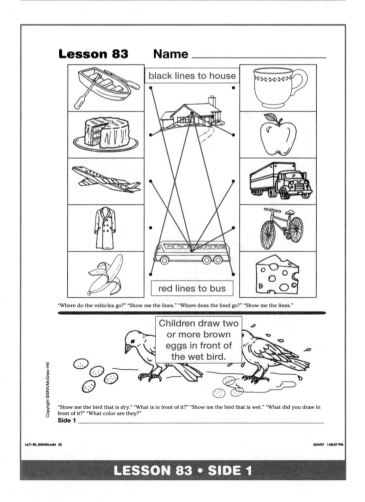

Lesson 83   Name _____

black lines to house

red lines to bus

"Where do the vehicles go?" "Show me the lines." "Where does the food go?" "Show me the lines."

Children draw two
or more brown
eggs in front of
the wet bird.

"Show me the bird that is dry." "What is in front of it?" "Show me the bird that is wet." "What did you draw in front of it?" "What color are they?"

Side 1 _____

LESSON 83 • SIDE 1

Lesson 83   Name _____

triangles: red
circles: blue
other objects:
  any color

Point to a circle. "What is this?" "What color is it?" Point to a triangle. "What is this?" "What color is it?"

Children draw
rectangles and
color them red.

Point to the shaded rectangle. "What is this?" Point to a red rectangle. "What did you draw?" "What color is it?"

Side 2 _____

LESSON 83 • SIDE 2

Lesson 84   Name _____

Children color wheels red on trucks that are not empty.

"Show me a truck that is not empty." "What color are the wheels?" "Show me another truck that is not empty." "What color are its wheels?"

Children make brown leaves on the tall tree.

"Show me the tree that is short." "Now show me the tree that is tall." "What did you draw on it?" "What color are they?"

Side 1 _____

LESSON 84 • SIDE 1

Lesson 84   Name _____

vehicles: blue
other objects: any color

"Point to an object that is food." "Point to another one." "Now point to an object that is a vehicle." "Point to another one."

Children circle the bird they want to fly. They color that bird black and cross out the birds that will not fly.

Side 2

L&71-85_809429.indd 89   8/94/07 1:09:59 PM

LESSON 84 • SIDE 2

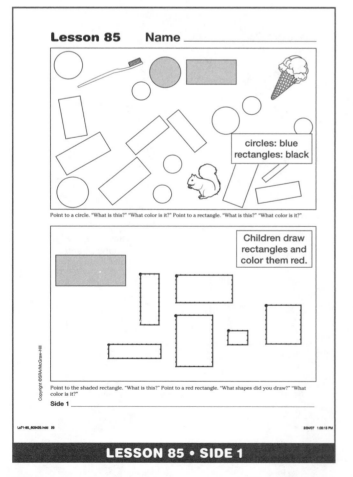

Lesson 85   Name _____

circles: blue
rectangles: black

Point to a circle. "What is this?" "What color is it?" Point to a rectangle. "What is this?" "What color is it?"

Children draw rectangles and color them red.

Point to the shaded rectangle. "What is this?" Point to a red rectangle. "What shapes did you draw?" "What color is it?"

Side 1 _____

Ls71-85_809429.indd 29   8/94/07 1:09:15 PM

LESSON 85 • SIDE 1

Lesson 85   Name _____

"Show me a duck that is big." "Show me a duck that is not big."

"Touch a box you circled." "What's in the box?" "Touch another box you circled." "What's in the box?" "Touch a box you crossed out." "What's in the box?"

Side 2

Ls71-85_809429.indd 30   8/94/07 1:09:16 PM

LESSON 85 • SIDE 2

34

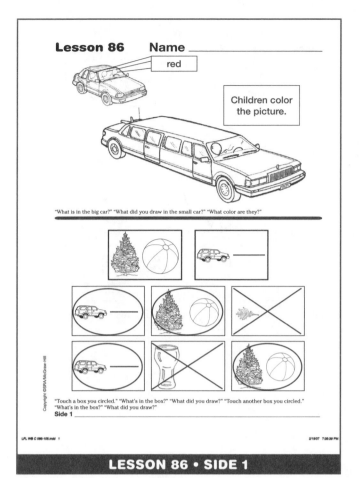

Lesson 86 Name _____

red

Children color the picture.

"What is in the big car?" "What did you draw in the small car?" "What color are they?"

"Touch a box you circled." "What's in the box?" "What did you draw?" "Touch another box you circled."
"What's in the box?" "What did you draw?"
Side 1 _____

Copyright ©SRA/McGraw-Hill

LFL WB C 086-105.indd 1   2/19/07 7:36:39 PM

LESSON 86 • SIDE 1

Lesson 86 Name _____

monkeys: any color

"Show me the monkey that is big." "Show me the monkey that is small."

circles: green

rectangles: yellow

other objects: any color

Point to a circle. "What is this?" "What color is it?" Point to a rectangle. "What is this?" "What color is it?"
Side 2 _____

Copyright ©SRA/McGraw-Hill

LFL WB C 086-105.indd 2   2/19/07 7:37:06 PM

LESSON 86 • SIDE 2

Lesson 87 Name _____

other objects: any color

bags: yellow

"What is in front of the old woman?" "What did you draw in front of the young woman?" "What color are they?"

vehicles: red
other objects: any color

"Touch some food." "Touch a vehicle." "Touch another food." "Touch another vehicle."
Side 1 _____

Copyright ©SRA/McGraw-Hill

LFL WB C 086-105.indd 3   2/19/07 7:37:11 PM

LESSON 87 • SIDE 1

Lesson 87 Name _____

house: any color

"Show me a black animal." "Where does it go?" "Show me a white animal." "Where does it go?"

"What shape did you draw?" "Show me how you drew it."
Side 2 _____

Copyright ©SRA/McGraw-Hill

LFL WB C 086-105.indd 4   2/19/07 7:37:18 PM

LESSON 87 • SIDE 2

35

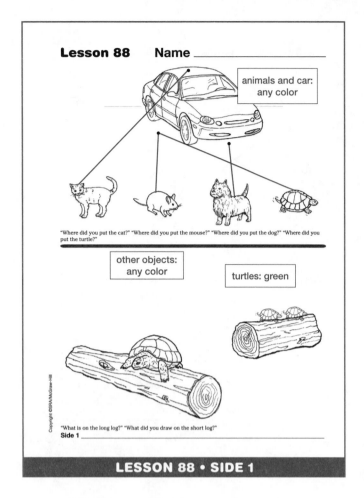

Lesson 88 Name _____

animals and car: any color

"Where did you put the cat?" "Where did you put the mouse?" "Where did you put the dog?" "Where did you put the turtle?"

other objects: any color

turtles: green

"What is on the long log?" "What did you draw on the short log?"
Side 1 _____

LESSON 88 • SIDE 1

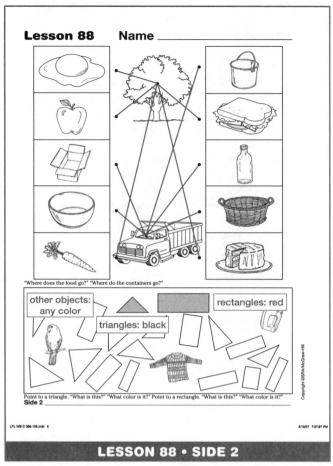

Lesson 88 Name _____

"Where does the food go?" "Where do the containers go?"

other objects: any color

triangles: black

rectangles: red

Point to a triangle. "What is this?" "What color is it?" Point to a rectangle. "What is this?" "What color is it?"
Side 2 _____

LFL WB C 086-105.indd 6   3/19/07 7:37:27 PM

LESSON 88 • SIDE 2

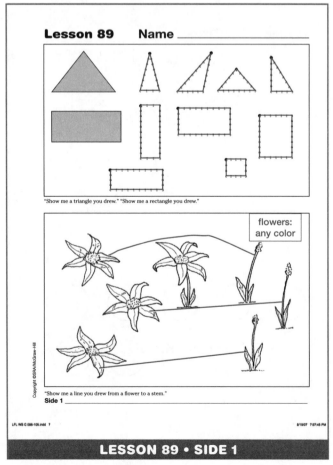

Lesson 89 Name _____

"Show me a triangle you drew." "Show me a rectangle you drew."

flowers: any color

"Show me a line you drew from a flower to a stem."
Side 1 _____

LFL WB C 086-105.indd 7   3/19/07 7:37:45 PM

LESSON 89 • SIDE 1

Lesson 89 Name _____

vehicles: green

foods: red

other objects: any color

Point to a vehicle. "What is it?" "What color is it?" Point to a food. "What is it?" "What color is it?"

animals and house: any color

"Tell me where you put the mouse." "Tell me where you put the cat." "Tell me where you put the squirrel." "Tell me where you put the bird."
Side 2 _____

LFL WB C 086-105.indd 8   3/19/07 7:37:48 PM

LESSON 89 • SIDE 2

36

Lesson 90　Name _____

Children color the picture.

"Tell me where you put the dog." "Tell me where you put the cat." "Tell me where you put the girl."

Children color the picture.

red flowers

"What is under the tall horse?" "What did you draw under the short horse?"
Side 1 _____

LFL WB C 090-105.indd　9　　2/19/07　7:38:10 PM

LESSON 90 • SIDE 1

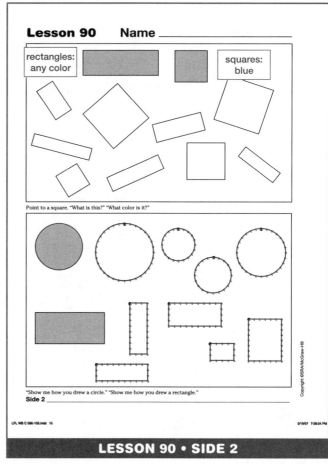

Lesson 90　Name _____

rectangles: any color

squares: blue

Point to a square. "What is this?" "What color is it?"

"Show me how you drew a circle." "Show me how you drew a rectangle."
Side 2 _____

LFL WB C 090-105.indd　10　　2/19/07　7:38:24 PM

LESSON 90 • SIDE 2

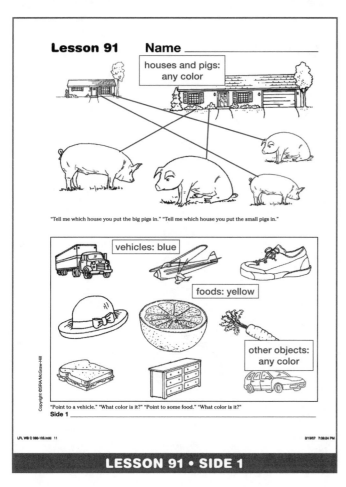

Lesson 91　Name _____

houses and pigs: any color

"Tell me which house you put the big pigs in." "Tell me which house you put the small pigs in."

vehicles: blue

foods: yellow

other objects: any color

"Point to a vehicle." "What color is it?" "Point to some food." "What color is it?"
Side 1 _____

LFL WB C 090-105.indd　11　　2/19/07　7:38:24 PM

LESSON 91 • SIDE 1

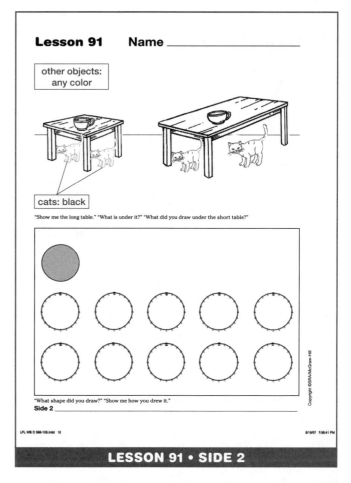

Lesson 91　Name _____

other objects: any color

cats: black

"Show me the long table." "What is under it?" "What did you draw under the short table?"

"What shape did you draw?" "Show me how you drew it."
Side 2 _____

LFL WB C 090-105.indd　12　　2/19/07　7:38:41 PM

LESSON 91 • SIDE 2

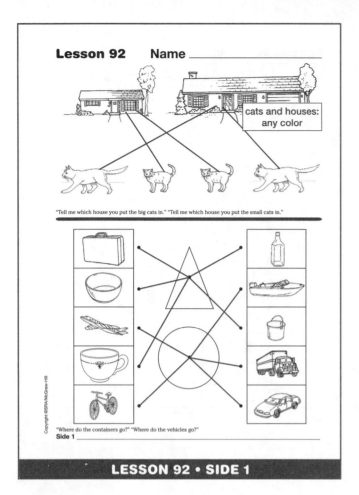

Lesson 92   Name _____

cats and houses: any color

"Tell me which house you put the big cats in." "Tell me which house you put the small cats in."

"Where do the containers go?" "Where do the vehicles go?"
Side 1 _____

LESSON 92 • SIDE 1

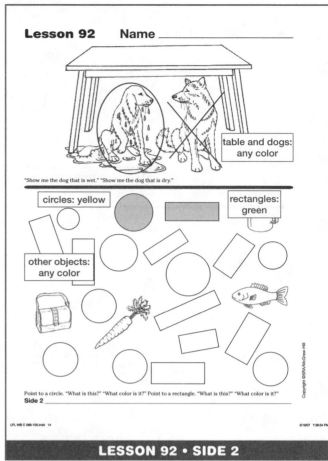

Lesson 92   Name _____

table and dogs: any color

"Show me the dog that is wet." "Show me the dog that is dry."

circles: yellow

rectangles: green

other objects: any color

Point to a circle. "What is this?" "What color is it?" Point to a rectangle. "What is this?" "What color is it?"
Side 2 _____

LFL WB C 086-105.indd 14   2/19/07 7:38:54 PM

LESSON 92 • SIDE 2

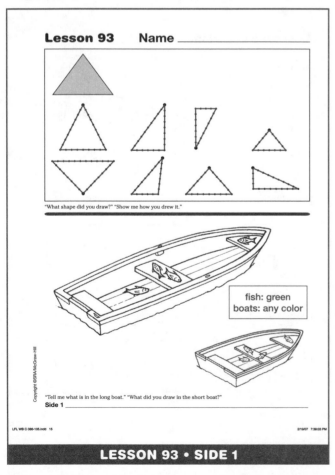

Lesson 93   Name _____

"What shape did you draw?" "Show me how you drew it."

fish: green
boats: any color

"Tell me what is in the long boat." "What did you draw in the short boat?"
Side 1 _____

LFL WB C 086-105.indd 15   2/19/07 7:39:03 PM

LESSON 93 • SIDE 1

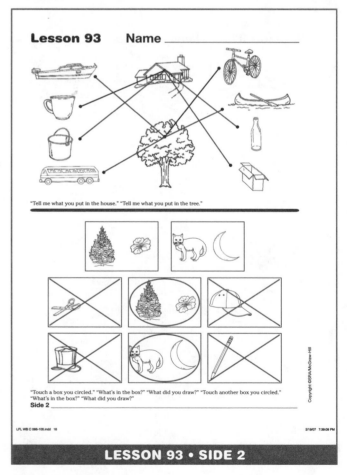

Lesson 93   Name _____

"Tell me what you put in the house." "Tell me what you put in the tree."

"Touch a box you circled." "What's in the box?" "What did you draw?" "Touch another box you circled."
"What's in the box?" "What did you draw?"
Side 2 _____

LFL WB C 086-105.indd 16   2/19/07 7:39:09 PM

LESSON 93 • SIDE 2

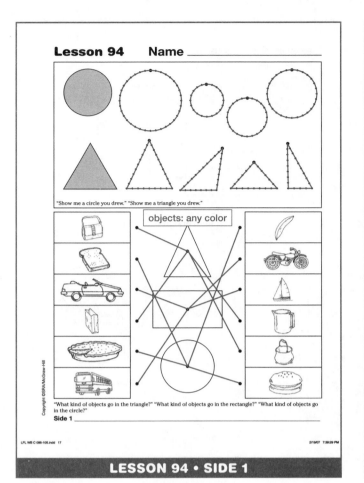

Lesson 94   Name _____

objects: any color

"Show me a circle you drew." "Show me a triangle you drew."

"What kind of objects go in the triangle?" "What kind of objects go in the rectangle?" "What kind of objects go in the circle?"
Side 1 _____

LFL WB C 086-105.indd   17   2/19/07   7:39:29 PM

LESSON 94 • SIDE 1

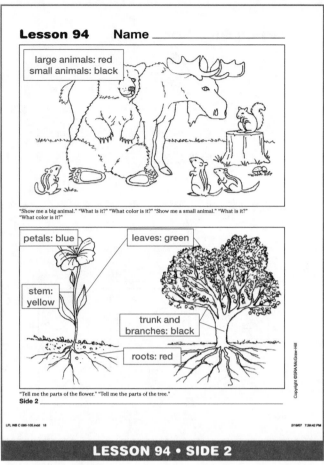

Lesson 94   Name _____

large animals: red
small animals: black

"Show me a big animal." "What is it?" "What color is it?" "Show me a small animal." "What color is it?"

petals: blue

leaves: green

stem: yellow

trunk and branches: black

roots: red

"Tell me the parts of the flower." "Tell me the parts of the tree."
Side 2 _____

LFL WB C 086-105.indd   18   2/19/07   7:39:42 PM

LESSON 94 • SIDE 2

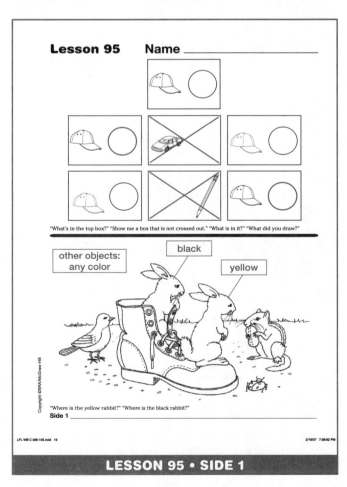

Lesson 95   Name _____

"What's in the top box?" "Show me a box that is not crossed out." "What is in it?" "What did you draw?"

other objects: any color

black

yellow

"Where is the yellow rabbit?" "Where is the black rabbit?"
Side 1 _____

LFL WB C 086-105.indd   19   2/19/07   7:39:52 PM

LESSON 95 • SIDE 1

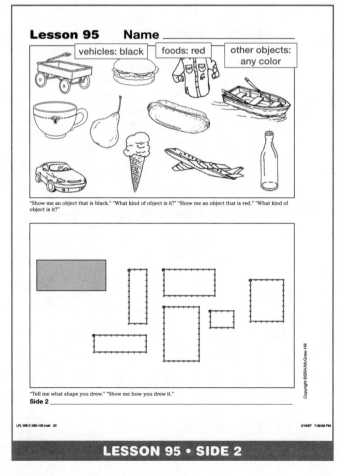

Lesson 95   Name _____

vehicles: black   foods: red   other objects: any color

"Show me an object that is black." "What kind of object is it?" "Show me an object that is red." "What kind of object is it?"

"Tell me what shape you drew." "Show me how you drew it."
Side 2 _____

LFL WB C 086-105.indd   20   2/19/07   7:39:56 PM

LESSON 95 • SIDE 2

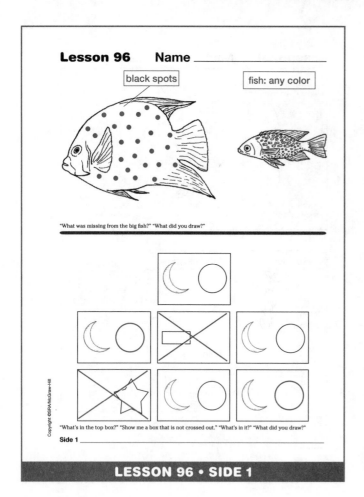

Lesson 96   Name _____

black spots

fish: any color

"What was missing from the big fish?" "What did you draw?"

"What's in the top box?" "Show me a box that is not crossed out." "What's in it?" "What did you draw?"

Side 1 _____

LESSON 96 • SIDE 1

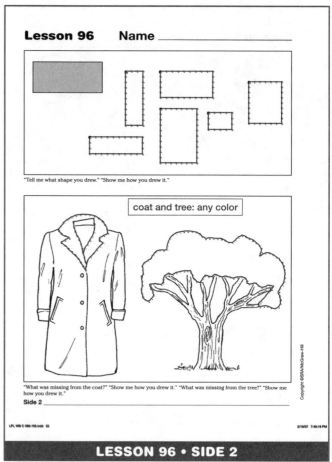

Lesson 96   Name _____

"Tell me what shape you drew." "Show me how you drew it."

coat and tree: any color

"What was missing from the coat?" "Show me how you drew it." "What was missing from the tree?" "Show me how you drew it."

Side 2 _____

LESSON 96 • SIDE 2

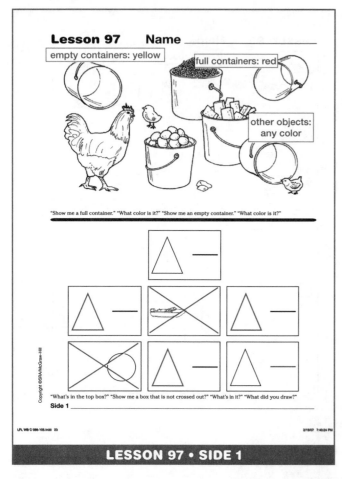

Lesson 97   Name _____

empty containers: yellow

full containers: red

other objects: any color

"Show me a full container." "What color is it?" "Show me an empty container." "What color is it?"

"What's in the top box?" "Show me a box that is not crossed out?" "What's in it?" "What did you draw?"

Side 1 _____

LESSON 97 • SIDE 1

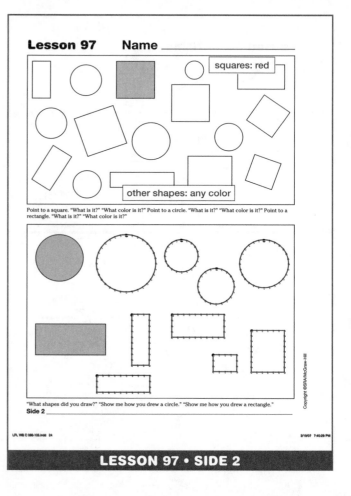

Lesson 97   Name _____

squares: red

other shapes: any color

Point to a square. "What is it?" "What color is it?" Point to a circle. "What is it?" "What color is it?" Point to a rectangle. "What is it?" "What color is it?"

"What shapes did you draw?" "Show me how you drew a circle." "Show me how you drew a rectangle."

Side 2 _____

LESSON 97 • SIDE 2

Lesson 98   Name _____

Children may add stripes or make all one color.

black spots

"What did you draw on the dry cat?" "Touch the other cat." "Is it wet or dry?"

long logs: green
short logs: yellow
all trees: brown
other objects: any color

"Show me a short log." "What color is it?" "Show me a long log." "What color is it?"

Side 1 _____

LESSON 98 • SIDE 1

Lesson 98   Name _____

other objects: any color

all containers: black
all foods: green

"What kind of objects did you color black?" "What kind of objects did you color green?"

"What shape did you draw?" "Show me how you drew it."

Side 2 _____

LESSON 98 • SIDE 2

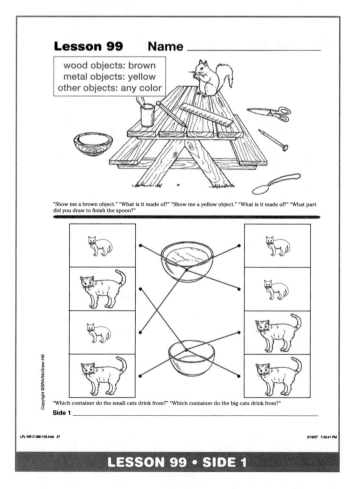

Lesson 99   Name _____

wood objects: brown
metal objects: yellow
other objects: any color

"Show me a brown object." "What is it made of?" "Show me a yellow object." "What is it made of?" "What part did you draw to finish the spoon?"

"Which container do the small cats drink from?" "Which container do the big cats drink from?"

Side 1 _____

LESSON 99 • SIDE 1

Lesson 99   Name _____

wet dogs: black
dry dogs: brown

"What color are the dry dogs?" "What color are the wet dogs?"

"What is in the circle?" "Which objects belong in the circle?"

Side 2 _____

LESSON 99 • SIDE 2

Lesson 100   Name _____

"What kind of objects go in the house?" "What kind of objects go in the circle?" "What kind of objects go in the triangle?"

wet horses: yellow
dry horses: black
other objects: any color

"What color are the dry horses?" "What color are the wet horses?"
Side 1 _____

LESSON 100 • SIDE 1

Lesson 100   Name _____

cloth objects: purple
plastic objects: red
other objects: any color

"What kind of objects did you color purple?" "What kind did you color red?" "What did you draw to finish the shirt?"

"What is in the circle?" "Tell me which objects belong in the circle."
Side 2 _____

LFL WB C 086-105.indd 30   2/19/07 7:41:15 PM

LESSON 100 • SIDE 2

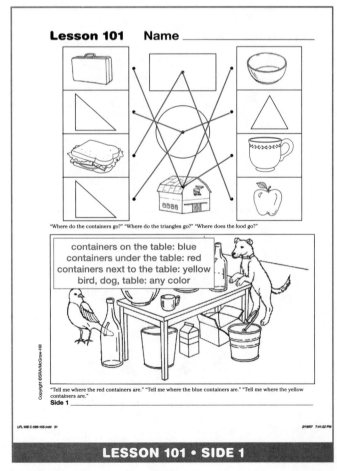

Lesson 101   Name _____

"Where do the containers go?" "Where do the triangles go?" "Where does the food go?"

containers on the table: blue
containers under the table: red
containers next to the table: yellow
bird, dog, table: any color

"Tell me where the red containers are." "Tell me where the blue containers are." "Tell me where the yellow containers are."
Side 1 _____

LFL WB C 086-105.indd 31   2/19/07 7:41:22 PM

LESSON 101 • SIDE 1

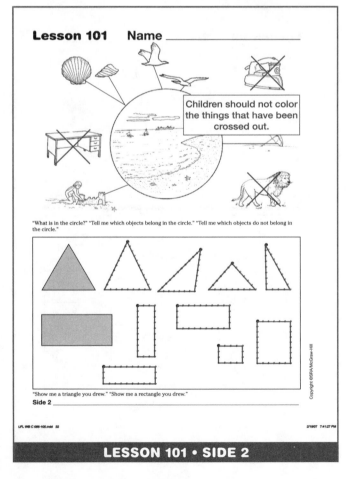

Lesson 101   Name _____

Children should not color the things that have been crossed out.

"What is in the circle?" "Tell me which objects belong in the circle." "Tell me which objects do not belong in the circle."

"Show me a triangle you drew." "Show me a rectangle you drew."
Side 2 _____

LFL WB C 086-105.indd 32   2/19/07 7:41:27 PM

LESSON 101 • SIDE 2

Lesson 102   Name

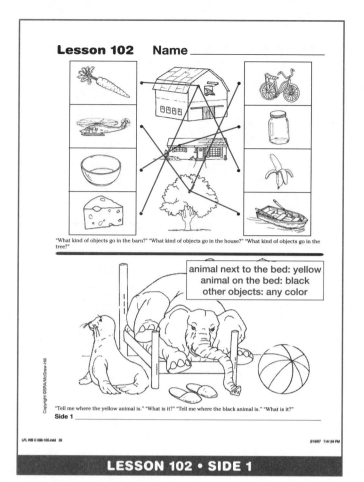

"What kind of objects go in the barn?" "What kind of objects go in the house?" "What kind of objects go in the tree?"

animal next to the bed: yellow
animal on the bed: black
other objects: any color

"Tell me where the yellow animal is." "What is it?" "Tell me where the black animal is." "What is it?"

Side 1 _____

LESSON 102 • SIDE 1

Lesson 102   Name

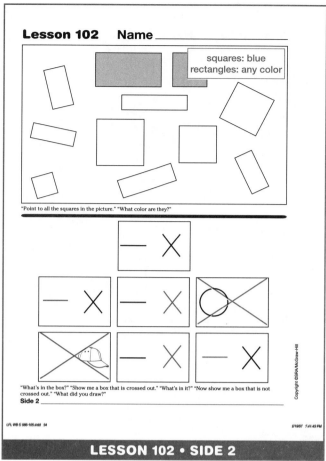

squares: blue
rectangles: any color

"Point to all the squares in the picture." "What color are they?"

"What's in the box?" "Show me a box that is crossed out." "What's in it?" "Now show me a box that is not crossed out." "What did you draw?"

Side 2 _____

LESSON 102 • SIDE 2

Lesson 103   Name

vehicles: red
animals: yellow

"What color are the vehicles?" "What color are the animals?"

"What's in the top box?" "Show me a box that is crossed out." "What's in it?" "Now show me a box that is not crossed out." "What did you draw?"

Side 1 _____

LESSON 103 • SIDE 1

Lesson 103   Name

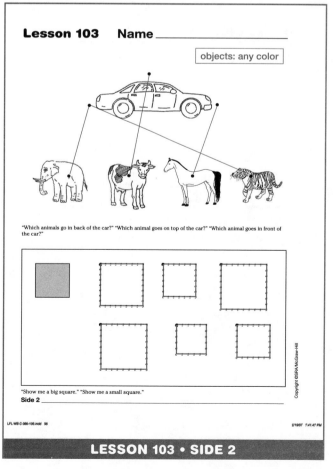

objects: any color

"Which animals go in back of the car?" "Which animal goes on top of the car?" "Which animal goes in front of the car?"

"Show me a big square." "Show me a small square."

Side 2 _____

LESSON 103 • SIDE 2

Lesson 104   Name _____

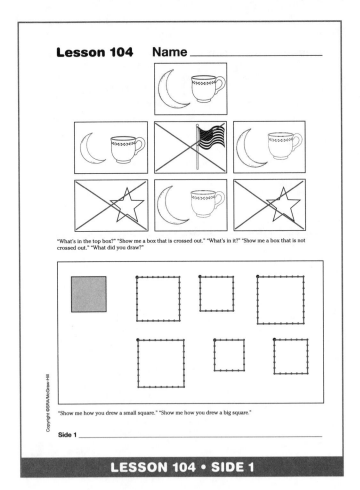

"What's in the top box?" "Show me a box that is crossed out." "What's in it?" "Show me a box that is not crossed out." "What did you draw?"

"Show me how you drew a small square." "Show me how you drew a big square."

Side 1 _____

LESSON 104 • SIDE 1

Lesson 104   Name _____

wet dogs: yellow
dry dogs: black

"What color are the wet dogs?" "What color are the dry dogs?"

things made of wood: any color

"Show me something that is made of wood." "What is it?" "Show me something that is not made of wood." "What is it?"

Side 2 _____

LESSON 104 • SIDE 2

Lesson 105   Name _____

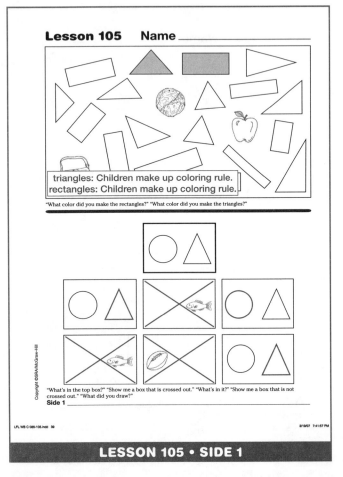

triangles: Children make up coloring rule.
rectangles: Children make up coloring rule.

"What color did you make the rectangles?" "What color did you make the triangles?"

"What's in the top box?" "Show me a box that is crossed out." "What's in it?" "Show me a box that is not crossed out." "What did you draw?"
Side 1 _____

LESSON 105 • SIDE 1

Lesson 105   Name _____

full containers: yellow
empty containers: red
animals: any color

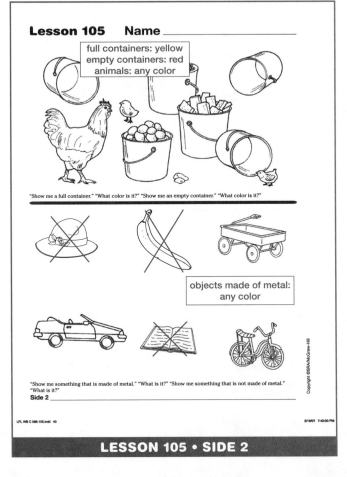

"Show me a full container." "What color is it?" "Show me an empty container." "What color is it?"

objects made of metal:
any color

"Show me something that is made of metal." "What is it?" "Show me something that is not made of metal." "What is it?"
Side 2 _____

LESSON 105 • SIDE 2

Lesson 106 Name _____

buildings: blue
vehicles: red
other objects: any color

"What color are the buildings?" "What color are the vehicles?"

rectangles: blue
other objects:
any color

"Show me how you drew the missing parts of the rectangles." "What color are they?"
Side 1 _____

Copyright ©SRA/McGraw-Hill

LESSON 106 • SIDE 1

Lesson 106 Name _____

boys and other objects:
any color

yellow   black   yellow

"What color is the animal that's between the boys?" "What is it?" "What color are the animals that are behind the boys?" "What are they?"

objects made of cloth: any color

"Show me something that's made of cloth." "What is it?" "Show me something that is not made of cloth." "What is it?"
Side 2 _____

Copyright ©SRA/McGraw-Hill

LESSON 106 • SIDE 2

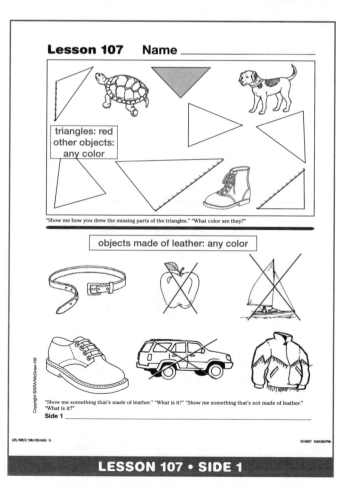

Lesson 107 Name _____

triangles: red
other objects:
any color

"Show me how you drew the missing parts of the triangles." "What color are they?"

objects made of leather: any color

"Show me something that's made of leather." "What is it?" "Show me something that's not made of leather." "What is it?"
Side 1 _____

Copyright ©SRA/McGraw-Hill

LESSON 107 • SIDE 1

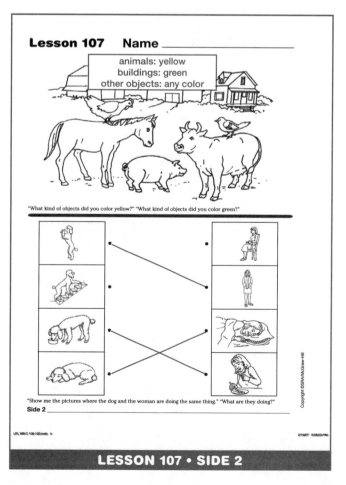

Lesson 107 Name _____

animals: yellow
buildings: green
other objects: any color

"What kind of objects did you color yellow?" "What kind of objects did you color green?"

"Show me the pictures where the dog and the woman are doing the same thing." "What are they doing?"
Side 2 _____

Copyright ©SRA/McGraw-Hill

LESSON 107 • SIDE 2

45

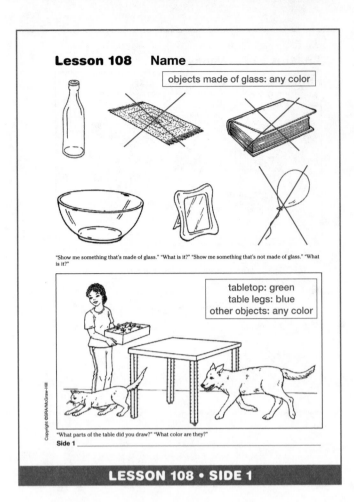

objects made of glass: any color

"Show me something that's made of glass." "What is it?" "Show me something that's not made of glass." "What is it?"

tabletop: green
table legs: blue
other objects: any color

"What parts of the table did you draw?" "What color are they?"
Side 1 _____

Copyright ©SRA/McGraw-Hill

LESSON 108 • SIDE 1

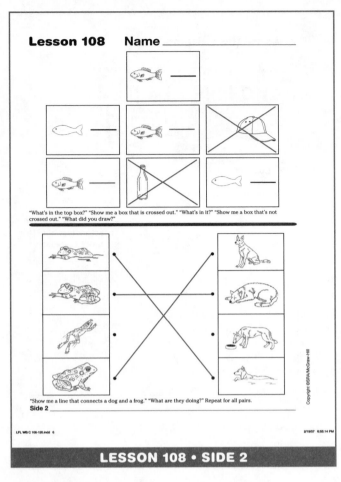

Lesson 108   Name

"What's in the top box?" "Show me a box that is crossed out." "What's in it?" "Show me a box that's not crossed out." "What did you draw?"

"Show me a line that connects a dog and a frog." "What are they doing?" Repeat for all pairs.
Side 2

LFL WB C 106-120.indd 6   2/19/07 6:55:14 PM

Copyright ©SRA/McGraw-Hill

LESSON 108 • SIDE 2

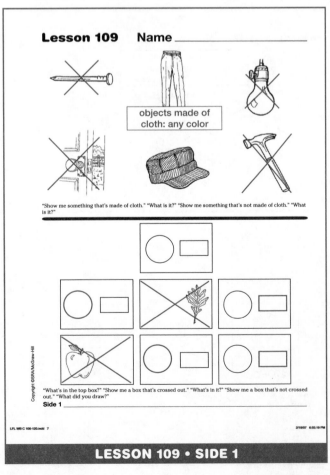

Lesson 109   Name

objects made of
cloth: any color

"Show me something that's made of cloth." "What is it?" "Show me something that's not made of cloth." "What is it?"

"What's in the top box?" "Show me a box that's crossed out." "What's in it?" "Show me a box that's not crossed out." "What did you draw?"
Side 1 _____

Copyright ©SRA/McGraw-Hill

LFL WB C 106-120.indd 7   2/19/07 6:55:19 PM

LESSON 109 • SIDE 1

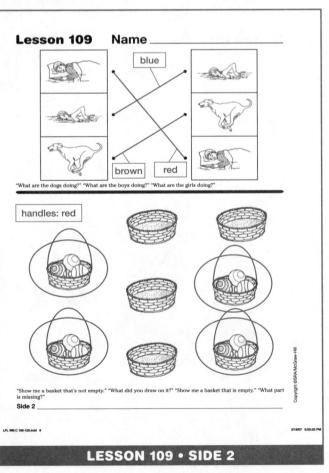

Lesson 109   Name

blue

brown   red

"What are the dogs doing?" "What are the boys doing?" "What are the girls doing?"

handles: red

"Show me a basket that's not empty." "What did you draw on it?" "Show me a basket that is empty." "What part is missing?"
Side 2 _____

Copyright ©SRA/McGraw-Hill

LFL WB C 106-120.indd 8   2/19/07 6:55:22 PM

LESSON 109 • SIDE 2

Lesson 110   Name _____

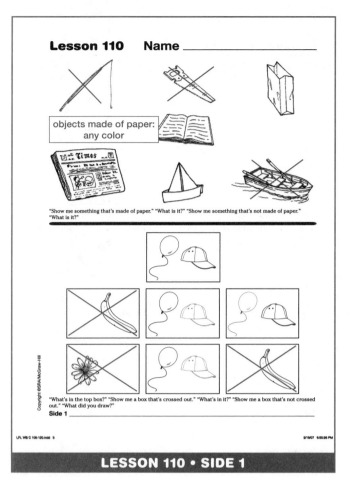

objects made of paper: any color

"Show me something that's made of paper." "What is it?" "Show me something that's not made of paper."
"What is it?"

"What's in the top box?" "Show me a box that's crossed out." "What's in it?" "Show me a box that's not crossed
out." "What did you draw?"
Side 1 _____

LESSON 110 • SIDE 1

Lesson 110   Name _____

birds on the dog: green
bird over the dog: blue
other objects: any color

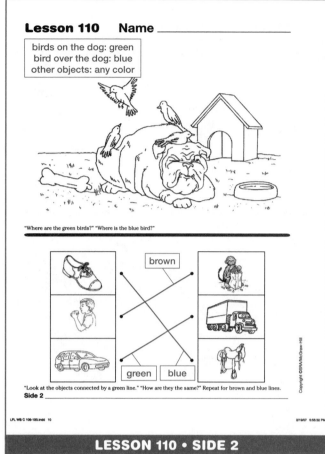

"Where are the green birds?" "Where is the blue bird?"

brown

green   blue

"Look at the objects connected by a green line." "How are they the same?" Repeat for brown and blue lines.
Side 2 _____

LESSON 110 • SIDE 2

Lesson 111   Name _____

objects made of wood: any color

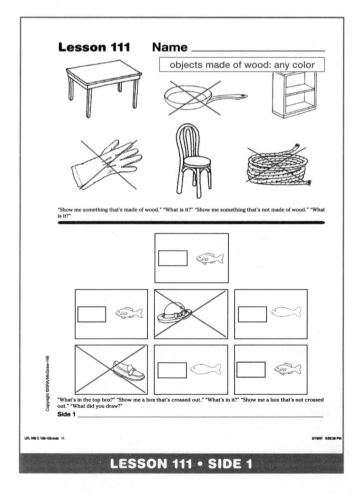

"Show me something that's made of wood." "What is it?" "Show me something that's not made of wood." "What
is it?"

"What's in the top box?" "Show me a box that's crossed out." "What's in it?" "Show me a box that's not crossed
out." "What did you draw?"
Side 1 _____

LESSON 111 • SIDE 1

Lesson 111   Name _____

buildings: blue
plants: green
other objects: any color

"Tell me what you colored blue." "Tell me what you colored green."

tall trees: brown
short trees: green
other objects: any color

"What color are the tall trees?" "What color are the short trees?"
Side 2 _____

LESSON 111 • SIDE 2

Lesson 112 Name _____

orange

red

black

any color

"Which animal is black?" "Which animal is red?" "Which animal is orange?" "What is the other animal?"

containers: red
plants: yellow
other objects: any color

"Show me the containers." "What color are they?" "Show me the plants." "What color are they?"
Side 1 _____

LESSON 112 • SIDE 1

Lesson 112 Name _____

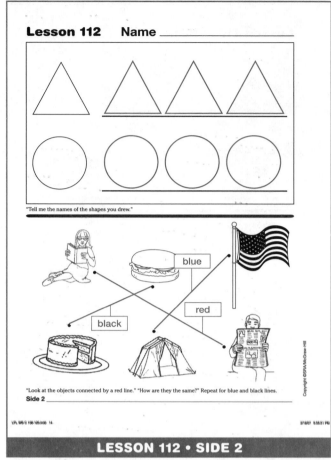

"Tell me the names of the shapes you drew."

blue

black

red

"Look at the objects connected by a red line." "How are they the same?" Repeat for blue and black lines.
Side 2

LESSON 112 • SIDE 2

Lesson 113 Name _____

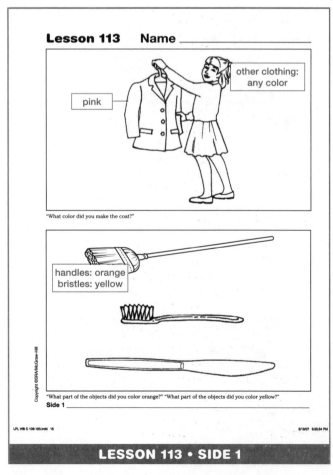

other clothing:
any color

pink

"What color did you make the coat?"

handles: orange
bristles: yellow

"What part of the objects did you color orange?" "What part of the objects did you color yellow?"
Side 1 _____

LESSON 113 • SIDE 1

Lesson 113 Name _____

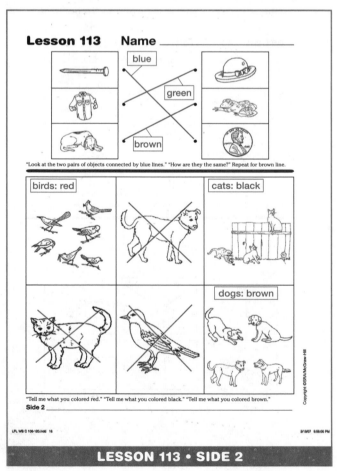

blue

green

brown

"Look at the two pairs of objects connected by blue lines." "How are they the same?" Repeat for brown line.

birds: red

cats: black

dogs: brown

"Tell me what you colored red." "Tell me what you colored black." "Tell me what you colored brown."
Side 2 _____

LESSON 113 • SIDE 2

Lesson 114   Name _____

pink · orange · brown · any color

"What color is the rabbit?" "What color is the lion?" "What color is the bear?" "What is the other animal?"

"Is the boy wearing glasses sad?" "Is the dog with the long tail big?"

Side 1 _____

LFL WB C 106-120.indd 17   2/19/07 6:56:19 PM

LESSON 114 • SIDE 1

Lesson 114   Name _____

uniforms: black
fire truck: red
fire pole: yellow
axe: green

"What did you color black?" "What did you color green?" "What did you color yellow?" "What did you color red?"

"Tell me what's in the top two boxes." "Tell me what you drew to fix the other boxes."

Side 2 _____

LESSON 114 • SIDE 2

Lesson 115   Name _____

green · blue · pink

table and cup: any color

"What color is the bowl?" "What color is the glass?" "What color is the plate?" "What else is on the table?"

"Tell me what's in the top two boxes." "Tell me what you drew to fix the other boxes."

Side 1 _____

LFL WB C 106-120.indd 19   2/19/07 6:56:41 PM

LESSON 115 • SIDE 1

Lesson 115   Name _____

circles: Children make up coloring rule.
rectangles: Children make up coloring rule.

"What rule did you make for rectangles?" "What rule did you make for circles?"

brown · green · blue

"Look at the objects connected by a brown line." "How are they the same?" Repeat for green and blue lines.

Side 2 _____

LFL WB C 106-120.indd 20   2/19/07 6:56:49 PM

LESSON 115 • SIDE 2

Lesson 116   Name _____

other objects: any color

body: blue

handle: red

wheels: black

"What was missing from the wagon?" "What part of the wagon is blue?" "What part is black?"

sun: yellow
sky: blue
ball: black
other objects: any color

"Tell me what you colored blue." "Tell me what you colored yellow." "Tell me what you colored black."
Side 1 _____

LESSON 116 • SIDE 1

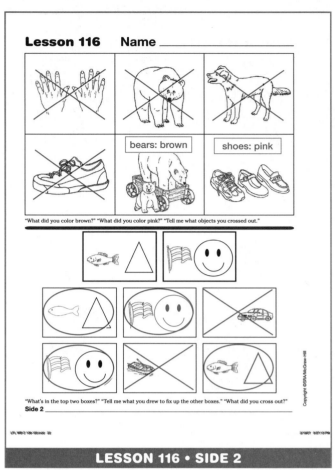

Lesson 116   Name _____

bears: brown

shoes: pink

"What did you color brown?" "What did you color pink?" "Tell me what objects you crossed out."

"What's in the top two boxes?" "Tell me what you drew to fix up the other boxes." "What did you cross out?"
Side 2 _____

LESSON 116 • SIDE 2

Lesson 117   Name _____

shirt: purple
other objects: any color

"What color did you make the boy's shirt?"

"What's in the top two boxes?" "Tell me what you drew to fix up the other boxes." "What did you cross out?"
Side 1 _____

LESSON 117 • SIDE 1

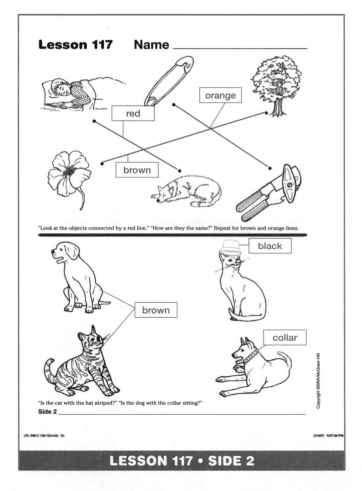

Lesson 117   Name _____

red

orange

brown

"Look at the objects connected by a red line." "How are they the same?" Repeat for brown and orange lines.

black

brown

collar

"Is the cat with the hat striped?" "Is the dog with the collar sitting?"
Side 2 _____

LESSON 117 • SIDE 2

Lesson 118 Name _____

rectangles: orange
other objects: any color

"What color are the rectangles?" "Show me how you followed the dots."

green

pink

any color

purple

"What color is the shoe?" "What color is the shirt?" "What color is the hat?" "What else is in the picture?"
Side 1 _____

LFL WB C 106-120.indd 25   2/19/07 6:57:55 PM

LESSON 118 • SIDE 1

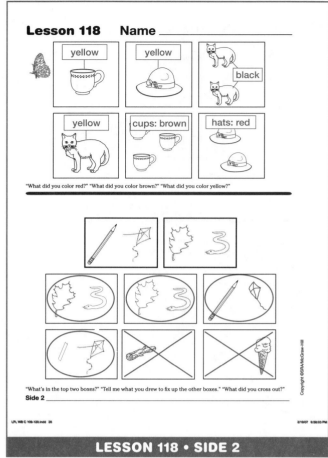

Lesson 118 Name _____

yellow

yellow

black

yellow

cups: brown

hats: red

"What did you color red?" "What did you color brown?" "What did you color yellow?"

"What's in the top two boxes?" "Tell me what you drew to fix up the other boxes." "What did you cross out?"
Side 2 _____

LFL WB C 106-120.indd 26   2/19/07 6:58:03 PM

LESSON 118 • SIDE 2

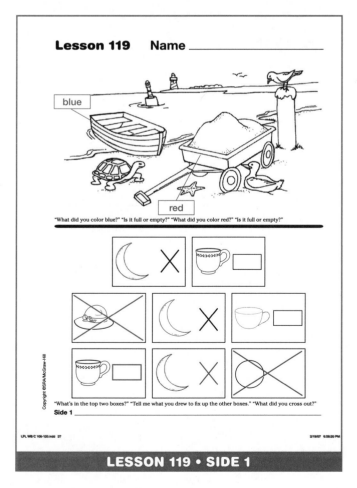

Lesson 119 Name _____

blue

red

"What did you color blue?" "Is it full or empty?" "What did you color red?" "Is it full or empty?"

"What's in the top two boxes?" "Tell me what you drew to fix up the other boxes." "What did you cross out?"
Side 1 _____

LFL WB C 106-120.indd 27   2/19/07 6:58:20 PM

LESSON 119 • SIDE 1

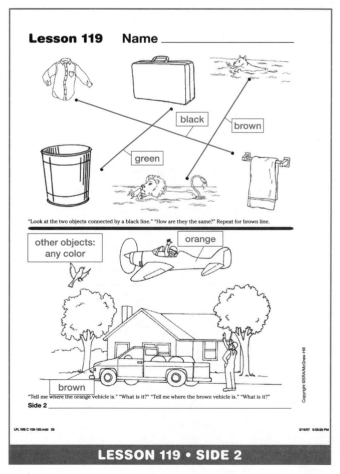

Lesson 119 Name _____

black

brown

green

"Look at the two objects connected by a black line." "How are they the same?" Repeat for brown line.

other objects:
any color

orange

brown

"Tell me where the orange vehicle is." "What is it?" "Tell me where the brown vehicle is." "What is it?"
Side 2 _____

LFL WB C 106-120.indd 28   2/19/07 6:58:29 PM

LESSON 119 • SIDE 2

Lesson 120　Name _____

yellow

brown

any color

purple

"What color is the table?" "What color is the chair?" "What color is the couch?" "What else is in the picture?"

other objects: any color

coat: red

"Is the woman in the red coat sitting?" "Is the box with a cross-out mark big?" "Is the cat next to the wagon wearing a collar?"
Side 1 _____

LESSON 120 • SIDE 1

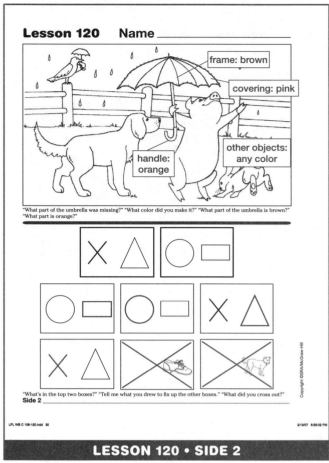

Lesson 120　Name _____

frame: brown

covering: pink

handle: orange

other objects: any color

"What part of the umbrella was missing?" "What color did you make it?" "What part of the umbrella is brown?" "What part is orange?"

"What's in the top two boxes?" "Tell me what you drew to fix up the other boxes." "What did you cross out?"
Side 2 _____

LESSON 120 • SIDE 2

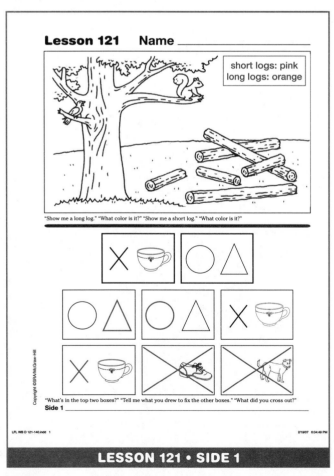

Lesson 121　Name _____

short logs: pink
long logs: orange

"Show me a long log." "What color is it?" "Show me a short log." "What color is it?"

"What's in the top two boxes?" "Tell me what you drew to fix up the other boxes." "What did you cross out?"
Side 1 _____

LESSON 121 • SIDE 1

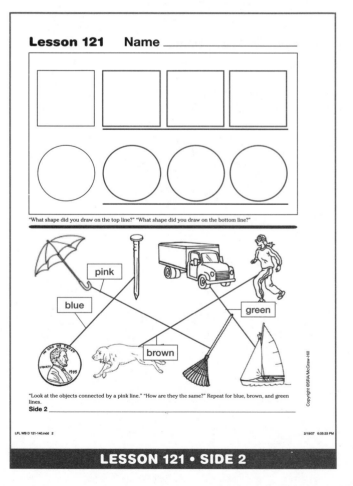

Lesson 121　Name _____

"What shape did you draw on the top line?" "What shape did you draw on the bottom line?"

pink

blue

green

brown

"Look at the objects connected by a pink line." "How are they the same?" Repeat for blue, brown, and green lines.
Side 2 _____

LESSON 121 • SIDE 2

Lesson 122   Name _____

foods: red
containers: green
other objects: any color

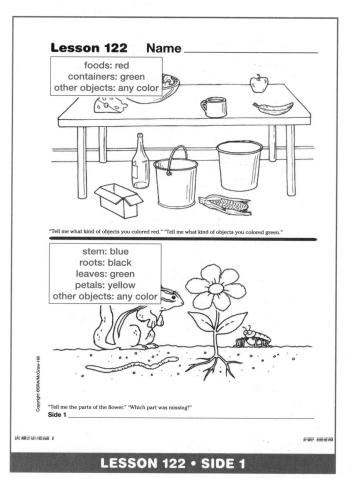

"Tell me what kind of objects you colored red." "Tell me what kind of objects you colored green."

stem: blue
roots: black
leaves: green
petals: yellow
other objects: any color

"Tell me the parts of the flower." "Which part was missing?"
Side 1 _____

LESSON 122 • SIDE 1

Lesson 122   Name _____

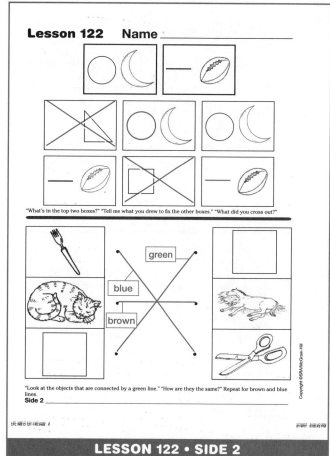

"What's in the top two boxes?" "Tell me what you drew to fix the other boxes." "What did you cross out?"

green
blue
brown

"Look at the objects that are connected by a green line." "How are they the same?" Repeat for brown and blue lines.
Side 2 _____

LESSON 122 • SIDE 2

Lesson 123   Name _____

Containers in circle: red line
vehicles in box: black line
clothing in wagon: green line

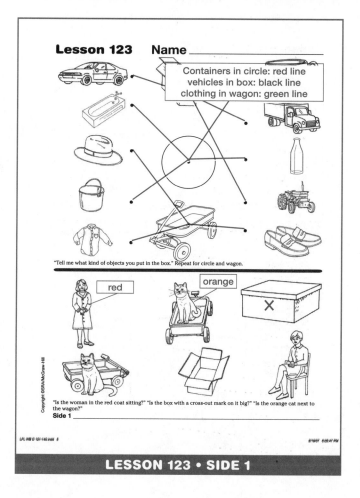

"Tell me what kind of objects you put in the box." Repeat for circle and wagon.

red
orange

"Is the woman in the red coat sitting?" "Is the box with a cross-out mark on it big?" "Is the orange cat next to the wagon?"
Side 1 _____

LESSON 123 • SIDE 1

Lesson 123   Name _____

collar: black
pockets: green
buttons: red
front: blue
sleeves: yellow
pants: any color

"Tell me the parts of the coat." "Which part was missing?"

clothing and buildings:
any color

"What kind of objects did you draw circles around?" "What kind of objects did you draw triangles around?" "What objects are left over?"
Side 2 _____

LESSON 123 • SIDE 2

53

Lesson 124   Name _____

vehicles: purple
animals: brown

"Tell me what kind of objects you colored purple." "Tell me what kind of objects you colored brown."

red

brown

black

"Does the lumberjack with the red jacket have a long axe?" "Are his boots short?" "Does the lumberjack with the black boots have a short axe?"
Side 1 _____

LESSON 124 • SIDE 1

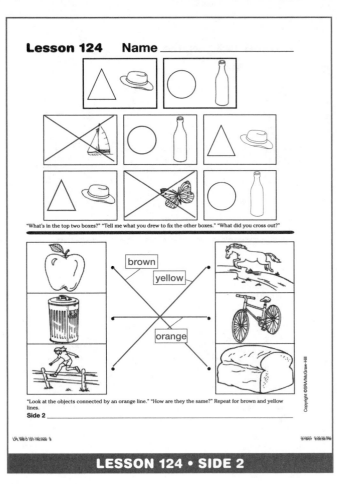

Lesson 124   Name _____

"What's in the top two boxes?" "Tell me what you drew to fix the other boxes." "What did you cross out?"

brown
yellow
orange

"Look at the objects connected by an orange line." "How are they the same?" Repeat for brown and yellow lines.
Side 2 _____

LESSON 124 • SIDE 2

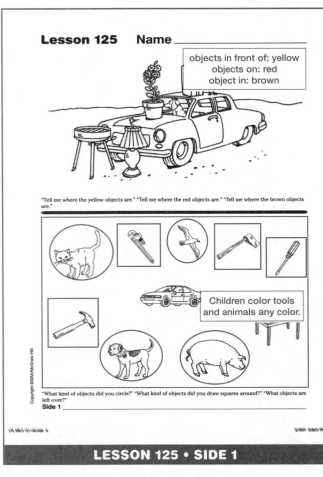

Lesson 125   Name _____

objects in front of: yellow
objects on: red
object in: brown

"Tell me where the yellow objects are." "Tell me where the red objects are." "Tell me where the brown objects are."

Children color tools
and animals any color.

"What kind of objects did you circle?" "What kind of objects did you draw squares around?" "What objects are left over?"
Side 1 _____

LESSON 125 • SIDE 1

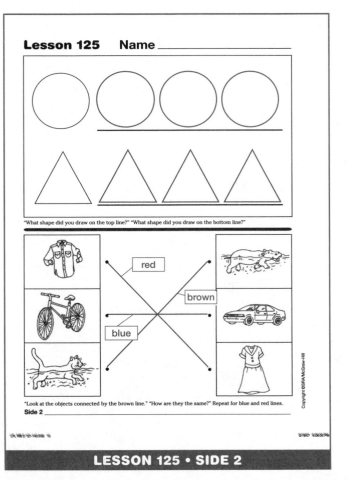

Lesson 125   Name _____

"What shape did you draw on the top line?" "What shape did you draw on the bottom line?"

red

blue

brown

"Look at the objects connected by the brown line." "How are they the same?" Repeat for blue and red lines.
Side 2 _____

LESSON 125 • SIDE 2

Lesson 126   Name _____

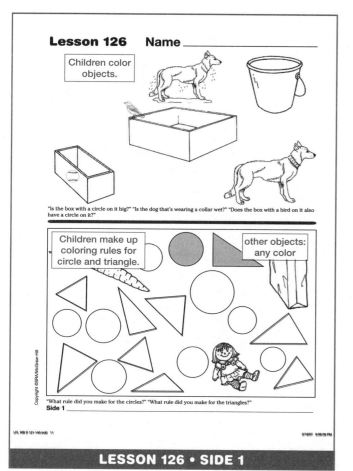

Children color objects.

"Is the box with a circle on it big?" "Is the dog that's wearing a collar wet?" "Does the box with a bird on it also have a circle on it?"

Children make up coloring rules for circle and triangle.

other objects: any color

"What rule did you make for the circles?" "What rule did you make for the triangles?"
Side 1 _____

LFL WB D 121-140.indd 11   2/18/07 6:08:09 PM

LESSON 126 • SIDE 1

Lesson 126   Name _____

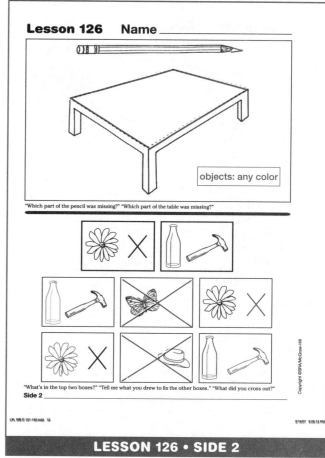

objects: any color

"Which part of the pencil was missing?" "Which part of the table was missing?"

"What's in the top two boxes?" "Tell me what you drew to fix the other boxes." "What did you cross out?"
Side 2 _____

LFL WB D 121-140.indd 12   2/18/07 6:08:12 PM

LESSON 126 • SIDE 2

Lesson 127   Name _____

tall trees: green
short trees: purple
other objects: any color

"What color are the tall trees?" "What color are the short trees?"

plants and containers: any color

"What kind of objects did you draw rectangles around?" "What kind of objects did you draw triangles around?"
Side 1 _____

LFL WB D 121-140.indd 13   2/18/07 6:08:17 PM

LESSON 127 • SIDE 1

Lesson 127   Name _____

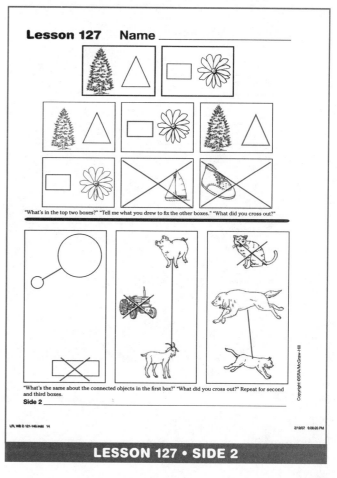

"What's in the top two boxes?" "Tell me what you drew to fix the other boxes." "What did you cross out?"

"What's the same about the connected objects in the first box?" "What did you cross out?" Repeat for second and third boxes.
Side 2 _____

LFL WB D 121-140.indd 14   2/18/07 6:08:20 PM

LESSON 127 • SIDE 2

Lesson 128 Name _____

Children color rest of picture.

black

green

brown

"Does the lumberjack wearing green pants have a long axe?" "Is the lumberjack with the black jacket wearing short boots?" "Does the lumberjack with brown boots have a long axe?"

Children make up coloring rules for rectangle and triangle.
other objects: any color

"What rule did you make for the rectangles?" "What rule did you make for the triangles?"
Side 1 _____

LESSON 128 • SIDE 1

Lesson 128 Name _____

walls: yellow
windows: black
door: green
roof: red

"Tell me the parts of the house." "Which part was missing?"

birds on: blue
birds over: red
other objects: any color

Children cross out one bird.

"Where are the blue birds?" "How many birds are next to the car?" "Where are the red birds?"
Side 2 _____

LESSON 128 • SIDE 2

Lesson 129 Name _____

food: orange
vehicles: brown
other objects: any color

"What kind of objects did you color orange?" "What kind of objects did you color brown?"

shoe top: purple
tongue: pink
sole: brown
laces: orange
heel: black

"Tell me the parts of the shoe." "Which part was missing?"
Side 1 _____

LESSON 129 • SIDE 1

Lesson 129 Name _____

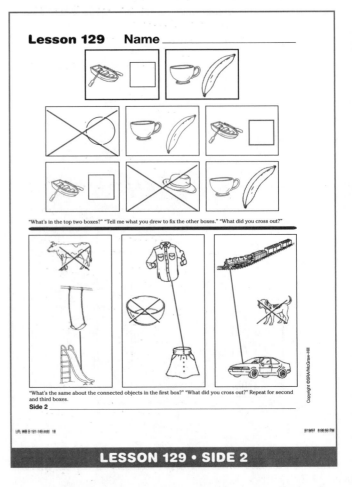

"What's in the top two boxes?" "Tell me what you drew to fix the other boxes." "What did you cross out?"

"What's the same about the connected objects in the first box?" "What did you cross out?" Repeat for second and third boxes.
Side 2 _____

LESSON 129 • SIDE 2

56

Lesson 130 Name _____

taller animals: black
shorter animals: red

"What animals did you color black?" "What animals did you color red?"

Children color
objects.

"What kind of objects did you circle?" "What kind of objects did you draw squares around?"
Side 1 _____

LFL WB D 121-140.indd 19   3/19/07 8:06:56 PM

LESSON 130 • SIDE 1

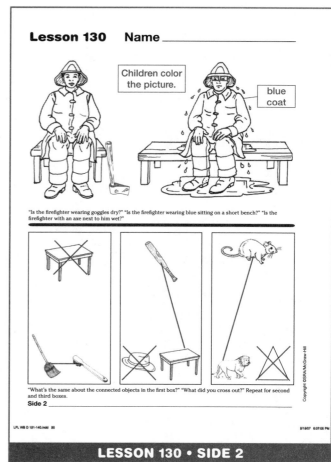

Lesson 130 Name _____

Children color
the picture.

blue
coat

"Is the firefighter wearing goggles dry?" "Is the firefighter wearing blue sitting on a short bench?" "Is the firefighter with an axe next to him wet?"

"What's the same about the connected objects in the first box?" "What did you cross out?" Repeat for second and third boxes.
Side 2 _____

LFL WB D 121-140.indd 20   3/19/07 8:07:05 PM

LESSON 130 • SIDE 2

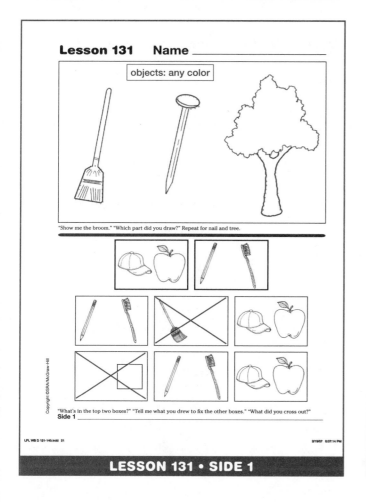

Lesson 131 Name _____

objects: any color

"Show me the broom." "Which part did you draw?" Repeat for nail and tree.

"What's in the top two boxes?" "Tell me what you drew to fix the other boxes." "What did you cross out?"
Side 1 _____

LFL WB D 121-140.indd 21   3/19/07 8:07:14 PM

LESSON 131 • SIDE 1

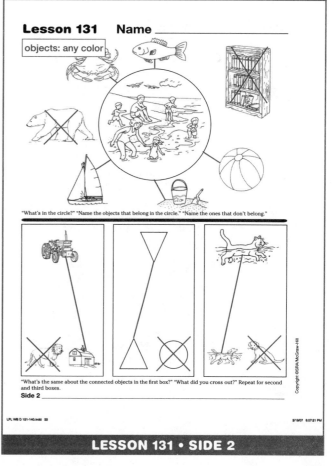

Lesson 131 Name _____

objects: any color

"What's in the circle?" "Name the objects that belong in the circle." "Name the ones that don't belong."

"What's the same about the connected objects in the first box?" "What did you cross out?" Repeat for second and third boxes.
Side 2 _____

LFL WB D 121-140.indd 22   3/19/07 8:07:21 PM

LESSON 131 • SIDE 2

Lesson 132   Name _____

smaller containers: yellow
bigger containers: blue
other objects: any color

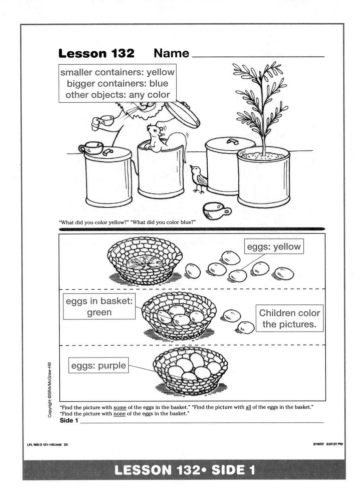

"What did you color yellow?" "What did you color blue?"

eggs: yellow

eggs in basket: green

Children color the pictures.

eggs: purple

"Find the picture with <u>some</u> of the eggs in the basket." "Find the picture with <u>all</u> of the eggs in the basket."
"Find the picture with <u>none</u> of the eggs in the basket."
Side 1 _____

LFL WB D 121-140.indd   23   2/19/07   6:07:27 PM

LESSON 132• SIDE 1

Lesson 132   Name _____

rungs: purple
back: brown
legs: orange
seat: pink

"Tell me the parts of the chair." "Which part was missing?"

objects made of wood: red
other objects: any color

"What kind of objects did you color red?"
Side 2 _____

LFL WB D 121-140.indd   24   2/19/07   6:07:43 PM

LESSON 132 • SIDE 2

Lesson 133   Name _____

dogs: with spots

Children color pictures.

dogs in doghouse: brown

dogs: black

"Find the picture with <u>all</u> of the dogs in the doghouse." "Find the picture with <u>none</u> of the dogs in the doghouse." "Find the picture with <u>some</u> of the dogs in the doghouse."

bristles: yellow
handle: black
other objects: any color

"Which part of the broom did you draw?"
Side 1 _____

LFL WB D 121-140.indd   25   2/19/07   6:07:48 PM

LESSON 133 • SIDE 1

Lesson 133   Name _____

pans: red
cats: brown
other objects: yellow

"Tell me which objects are red." "Tell me which are brown." "Tell me which are yellow."

"What's in the circle?" "Name the objects that belong in the circle." "Name the ones that don't belong."
Side 2 _____

LESSON 133 • SIDE 2

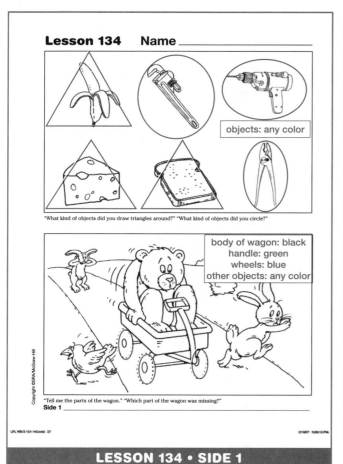

Lesson 134   Name _____

objects: any color

"What kind of objects did you draw triangles around?" "What kind of objects did you circle?"

body of wagon: black
handle: green
wheels: blue
other objects: any color

"Tell me the parts of the wagon." "Which part of the wagon was missing?"
Side 1 _____

LESSON 134 • SIDE 1

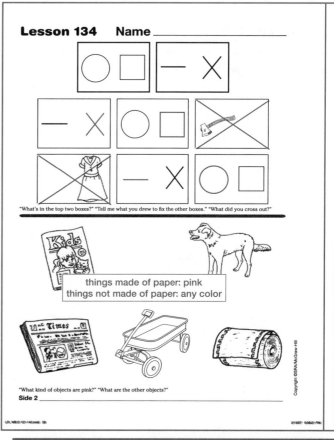

Lesson 134   Name _____

"What's in the top two boxes?" "Tell me what you drew to fix the other boxes." "What did you cross out?"

things made of paper: pink
things not made of paper: any color

"What kind of objects are pink?" "What are the other objects?"
Side 2 _____

LESSON 134 • SIDE 2

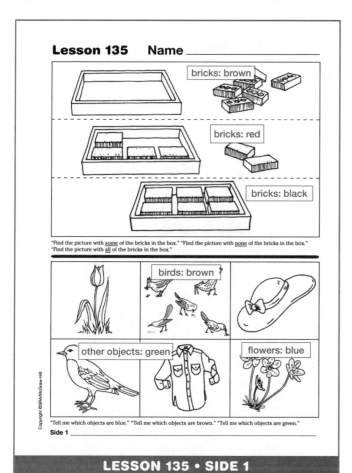

Lesson 135   Name _____

bricks: brown

bricks: red

bricks: black

"Find the picture with some of the bricks in the box." "Find the picture with none of the bricks in the box."
"Find the picture with all of the bricks in the box."

birds: brown

other objects: green

flowers: blue

"Tell me which objects are blue." "Tell me which objects are brown." "Tell me which objects are green."
Side 1 _____

LESSON 135 • SIDE 1

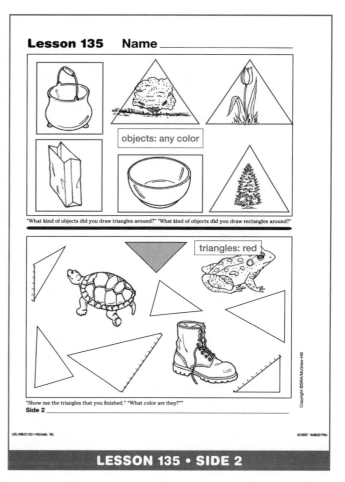

Lesson 135   Name _____

objects: any color

"What kind of objects did you draw triangles around?" "What kind of objects did you draw rectangles around?"

triangles: red

"Show me the triangles that you finished." "What color are they?"
Side 2 _____

LESSON 135 • SIDE 2

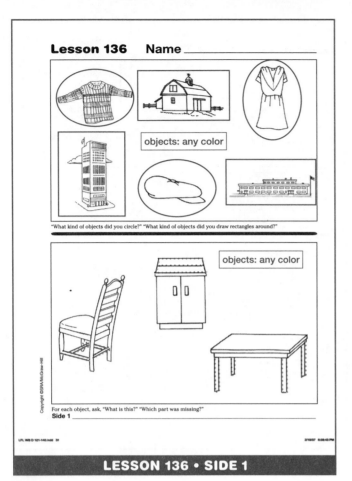

Lesson 136   Name _____

objects: any color

"What kind of objects did you circle?" "What kind of objects did you draw rectangles around?"

objects: any color

For each object, ask, "What is this?" "Which part was missing?"
Side 1 _____

LRL WB D 121-140.indd 31   2/19/07 6:08:43 PM

LESSON 136 • SIDE 1

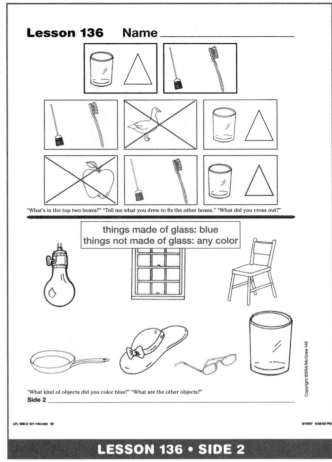

Lesson 136   Name _____

"What's in the top two boxes?" "Tell me what you drew to fix the other boxes." "What did you cross out?"

things made of glass: blue
things not made of glass: any color

"What kind of objects did you color blue?" "What are the other objects?"
Side 2 _____

LRL WB D 121-140.indd 32   2/19/07 6:08:50 PM

LESSON 136 • SIDE 2

Lesson 137   Name _____

eggs in basket:
some blue; some green

some cats: yellow

"Are all of the eggs in the basket?" "Are some of the eggs broken?" "Are all of the cats yellow?"

red

dogs and wet duck:
any color

"Is the red duck wet?" "Is the dog with a collar short?"
Side 1 _____

LRL WB D 121-140.indd 33   2/19/07 6:08:58 PM

LESSON 137 • SIDE 1

Lesson 137   Name _____

rectangles: yellow
other objects: any color

"Show me the rectangles that you finished." "What color are they?"

objects: any color

For each object, ask, "What is this?" "Which part was missing?"
Side 2 _____

LRL WB D 121-140.indd 34   2/19/07 6:09:14 PM

LESSON 137 • SIDE 2

Lesson 138   Name _____

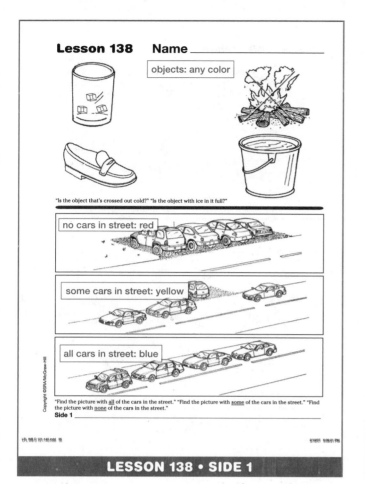

objects: any color

"Is the object that's crossed out cold?" "Is the object with ice in it full?"

no cars in street: red

some cars in street: yellow

all cars in street: blue

"Find the picture with all of the cars in the street." "Find the picture with some of the cars in the street." "Find the picture with none of the cars in the street."
Side 1 _____

LESSON 138 • SIDE 1

Lesson 138   Name _____

things made of leather: brown
things not made of leather: any color

"What kind of objects are brown?" "What are the other objects?"

hats: black
uniforms: brown
axe: blue
other objects: any color

"What place is in the picture?" "What did you color black?" "What did you color brown?" "What did you color blue?"
Side 2 _____

LESSON 138 • SIDE 2

Lesson 139   Name _____

some kittens not in box: black
all kittens in box: brown
puppies: not black

"Are some of the kittens black?" "Are they in the box?" "Are all of the kittens brown?" "Are they next to the box?" "Are all of the puppies black?"

Children color faces.

"Are the men sad?" "Are the women happy?"
Side 1 _____

LESSON 139 • SIDE 1

Lesson 139   Name _____

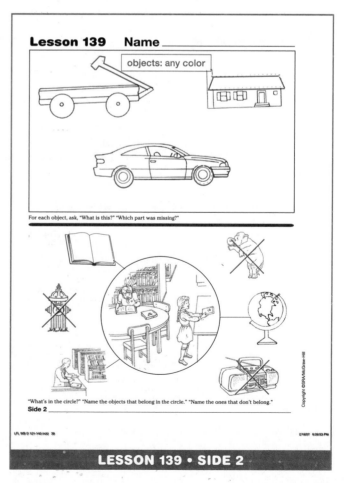

objects: any color

For each object, ask, "What is this?" "Which part was missing?"

"What's in the circle?" "Name the objects that belong in the circle." "Name the ones that don't belong."
Side 2 _____

LESSON 139 • SIDE 2

61

Lesson 140   Name _____

Children color children.

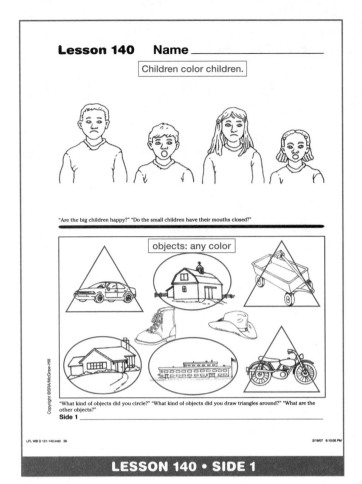

"Are the big children happy?" "Do the small children have their mouths closed?"

objects: any color

"What kind of objects did you circle?" "What kind of objects did you draw triangles around?" "What are the other objects?"
Side 1

LFL WB D 121-140.indd   39   2/19/07   6:10:05 PM

LESSON 140 • SIDE 1

Lesson 140   Name _____

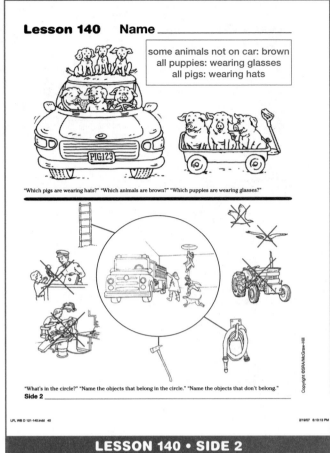

some animals not on car: brown
all puppies: wearing glasses
all pigs: wearing hats

PIG123

"Which pigs are wearing hats?" "Which animals are brown?" "Which puppies are wearing glasses?"

"What's in the circle?" "Name the objects that belong in the circle." "Name the objects that don't belong."
Side 2 _____

LFL WB D 121-140.indd   40   2/19/07   6:10:13 PM

LESSON 140 • SIDE 2

Lesson 141   Name _____

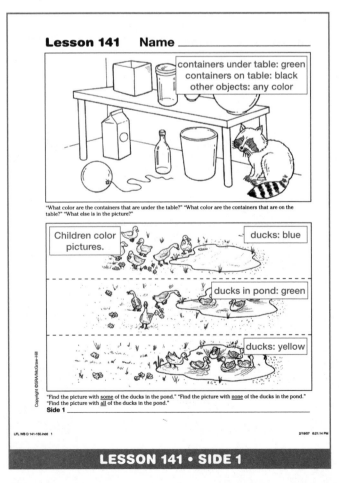

containers under table: green
containers on table: black
other objects: any color

"What color are the containers that are under the table?" "What color are the containers that are on the table?" "What else is in the picture?"

Children color pictures.

ducks: blue

ducks in pond: green

ducks: yellow

"Find the picture with some of the ducks in the pond." "Find the picture with none of the ducks in the pond." "Find the picture with all of the ducks in the pond."
Side 1 _____

LFL WB D 141-150.indd   1   2/19/07   6:21:14 PM

LESSON 141 • SIDE 1

Lesson 141   Name _____

Children color room.

black

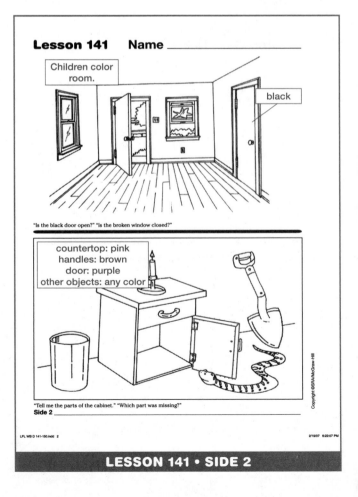

"Is the black door open?" "Is the broken window closed?"

countertop: pink
handles: brown
door: purple
other objects: any color

"Tell me the parts of the cabinet." "Which part was missing?"
Side 2 _____

LFL WB D 141-150.indd   2   2/19/07   6:22:07 PM

LESSON 141 • SIDE 2

Lesson 142   Name_____

goat and dog: black
turtle: brown

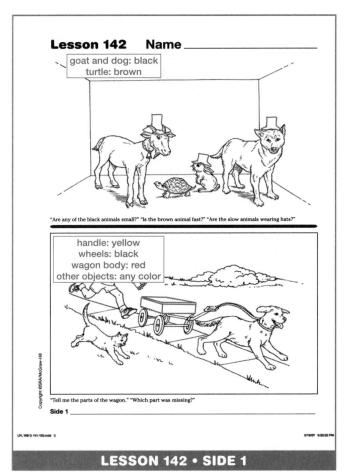

"Are any of the black animals small?" "Is the brown animal fast?" "Are the slow animals wearing hats?"

handle: yellow
wheels: black
wagon body: red
other objects: any color

"Tell me the parts of the wagon." "Which part was missing?"

Side 1 _____

LESSON 142 • SIDE 1

Lesson 142   Name_____

Children color jungle and objects.

"What's in the circle?" "Name the objects that belong in the circle." "Name the objects that don't belong."

"What's the same about the connected objects in the first box?" "What did you cross out?" Repeat for second and third boxes.

Side 2 _____

LESSON 142 • SIDE 2

Lesson 143   Name_____

"Are the wet boys sad?" "Are the dry boys happy?"

objects: any color

For each object, ask, "What is this?" "What part was missing?"

Side 1 _____

LESSON 143 • SIDE 1

Lesson 143   Name_____

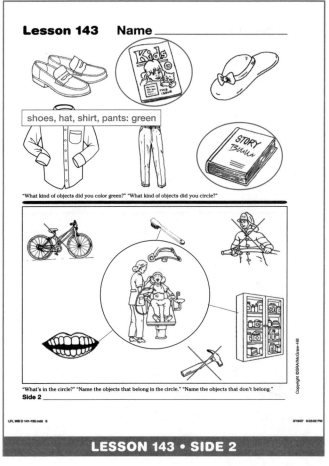

shoes, hat, shirt, pants: green

"What kind of objects did you color green?" "What kind of objects did you circle?"

"What's in the circle?" "Name the objects that belong in the circle." "Name the objects that don't belong."

Side 2 _____

LESSON 143 • SIDE 2

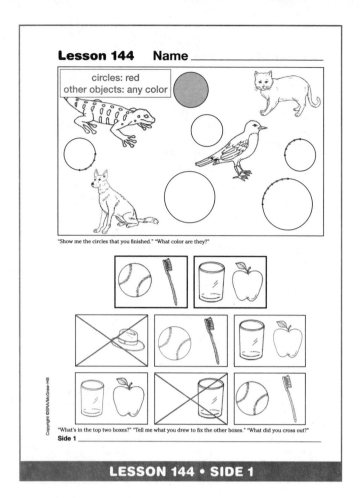

Lesson 144 Name _____

circles: red
other objects: any color

"Show me the circles that you finished." "What color are they?"

"What's in the top two boxes?" "Tell me what you drew to fix the other boxes." "What did you cross out?"
Side 1

LESSON 144 • SIDE 1

Lesson 144 Name _____

Children color forest and objects.

"What's in the circle?" "Name the objects that belong in the circle." "Name the ones that don't belong."

"What's the same about the connected objects in the first box?" "What did you cross out?" Repeat for second and third boxes.
Side 2 _____

LESSON 144 • SIDE 2

Lesson 145 Name _____

pockets: pink
collar: purple
front: orange
sleeves: green
buttons: yellow
other objects:
any color

"Tell me the parts of the coat." "Which part was missing?"

sheep, horse, cow, goat: brown

"What kind of objects are brown?" "What did you cross out?"
Side 1

LESSON 145 • SIDE 1

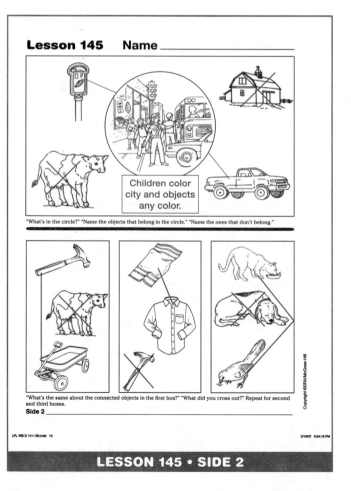

Lesson 145 Name _____

Children color city and objects any color.

"What's in the circle?" "Name the objects that belong in the circle." "Name the ones that don't belong."

"What's the same about the connected objects in the first box?" "What did you cross out?" Repeat for second and third boxes.
Side 2 _____

LESSON 145 • SIDE 2

Lesson 146   Name _____

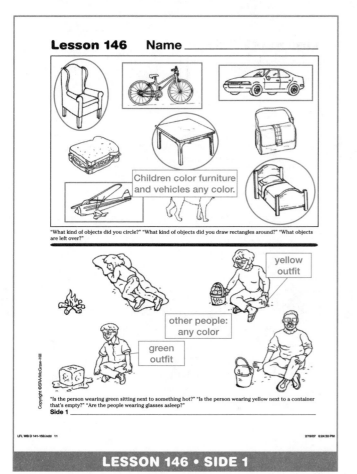

"What kind of objects did you circle?" "What kind of objects did you draw rectangles around?" "What objects are left over?"

yellow outfit

other people: any color

green outfit

"Is the person wearing green sitting next to something hot?" "Is the person wearing yellow next to a container that's empty?" "Are the people wearing glasses asleep?"
Side 1 _____

LFL WB D 141-150.indd 11   2/19/07 6:24:30 PM

LESSON 146 • SIDE 1

Lesson 146   Name _____

belt, shoe, glove, billfold: brown

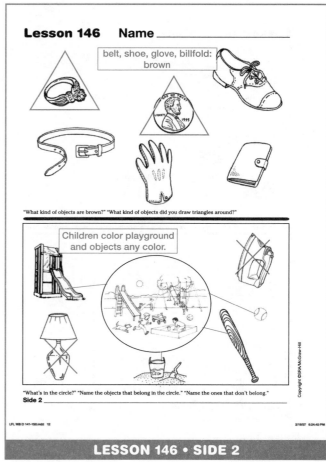

"What kind of objects are brown?" "What kind of objects did you draw triangles around?"

Children color playground and objects any color.

"What's in the circle?" "Name the objects that belong in the circle." "Name the ones that don't belong."
Side 2 _____

LFL WB D 141-150.indd 12   2/19/07 6:24:42 PM

LESSON 146 • SIDE 2

Lesson 147   Name _____

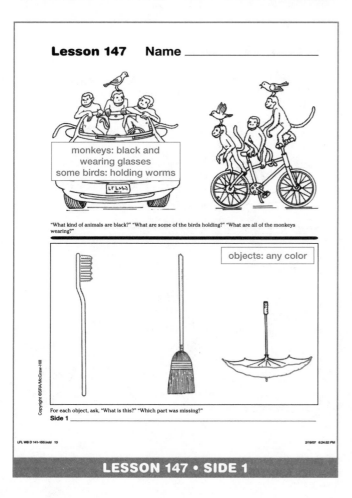

monkeys: black and wearing glasses
some birds: holding worms

"What kind of animals are black?" "What are some of the birds holding?" "What are all of the monkeys wearing?"

objects: any color

For each object, ask, "What is this?" "Which part was missing?"
Side 1 _____

LFL WB D 141-150.indd 13   2/19/07 6:24:52 PM

LESSON 147 • SIDE 1

Lesson 147   Name _____

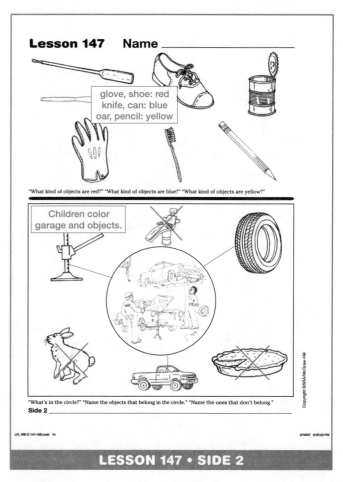

glove, shoe: red
knife, can: blue
oar, pencil: yellow

"What kind of objects are red?" "What kind of objects are blue?" "What kind of objects are yellow?"

Children color garage and objects.

"What's in the circle?" "Name the objects that belong in the circle." "Name the ones that don't belong."
Side 2 _____

LFL WB D 141-150.indd 14   2/19/07 6:25:02 PM

LESSON 147 • SIDE 2

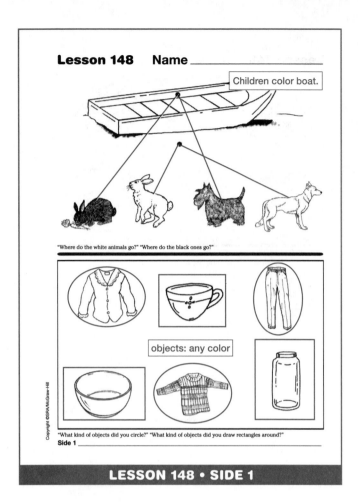

Lesson 148   Name _____

Children color boat.

"Where do the white animals go?" "Where do the black ones go?"

objects: any color

"What kind of objects did you circle?" "What kind of objects did you draw rectangles around?"
Side 1 _____

LESSON 148 • SIDE 1

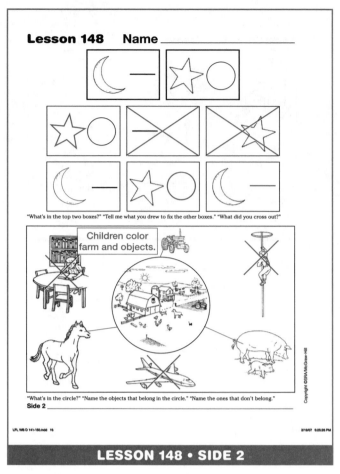

Lesson 148   Name _____

"What's in the top two boxes?" "Tell me what you drew to fix the other boxes." "What did you cross out?"

Children color farm and objects.

"What's in the circle?" "Name the objects that belong in the circle." "Name the ones that don't belong."
Side 2 _____

LESSON 148 • SIDE 2

Lesson 149   Name _____

some ducks: red
some ducks: blue
all boats: black

"Are all the blue animals in boats?" "Are all the red animals in boats?" "Are some of the animals with long whiskers wet?"

countertop: orange
doors: purple
handles: black

"Tell me the parts of the cabinet." "Which part was missing?"
Side 1 _____

LESSON 149 • SIDE 1

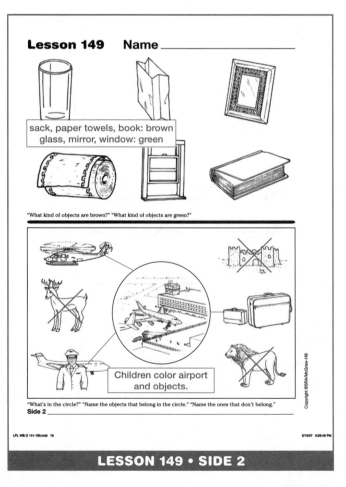

Lesson 149   Name _____

sack, paper towels, book: brown
glass, mirror, window: green

"What kind of objects are brown?" "What kind of objects are green?"

Children color airport and objects.

"What's in the circle?" "Name the objects that belong in the circle." "Name the ones that don't belong."
Side 2 _____

LESSON 149 • SIDE 2

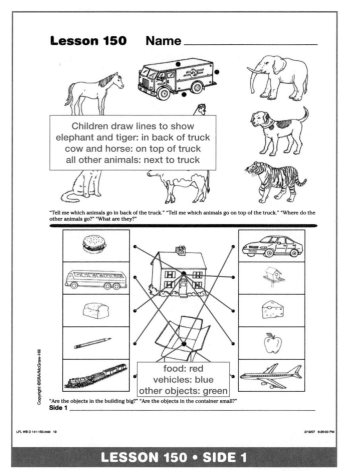

Lesson 150   Name _____

Children draw lines to show
elephant and tiger: in back of truck
cow and horse: on top of truck
all other animals: next to truck

"Tell me which animals go in back of the truck." "Tell me which animals go on top of the truck." "Where do the other animals go?" "What are they?"

food: red
vehicles: blue
other objects: green

"Are the objects in the building big?" "Are the objects in the container small?"
Side 1 _____

LFL WB D 141-150.indd   19   2/19/07 6:26:00 PM

Lesson 150   Name _____

some cats: black
vehicles: red
elephant: wet

"Is the wet animal small?" "What kind of objects are red?" "Are the black animals big?"

"What's in the top two boxes?" "Tell me what you drew to fix the other boxes." "What did you cross out?"
Side 2 _____

LFL WB D 141-150.indd   20   2/19/07 6:26:12 PM